Asperger's Syndrome *and* High Achievement

Asperger's Syndrome
and High Achievement

Some Very Remarkable People

Ioan James

Jessica Kingsley Publishers
London and Philadelphia

First published in 2006
by Jessica Kingsley Publishers
116 Pentonville Road
London N1 9JB, UK
and
400 Market Street, Suite 400
Philadelphia, PA 19106, USA

www.jkp.com

Library of Congress Cataloging in Publication Data
James, I. M. (Ioan Mackenzie), 1928-
 Asperger's syndrome and high achievement : some very remarkable people / Ioan James.
  p. cm.
 Includes bibliographical references and index.
 ISBN-13: 978-1-84310-388-2 (pbk. : alk. paper)
 ISBN-10: 1-84310-388-5 (pbk. : alk. paper) 1. Asperger's syndrome. 2. Genius and mental
illness. 3. Creative ability--Psychological aspects. 4. Asperger's syndrome--Patients--Biography. 5.
Autism--Patients--Biography. I. Title.

 RC553.A88J35 2006
 362.196'858832--dc22

                                                                    2005029311

British Library Cataloguing in Publication Data
A CIP catalogue record for this book is available from the British Library

ISBN-13: 978 1 84310 388 2
ISBN-10: 1 84310 388 5

Printed and bound in Great Britain by
Athenaeum Press, Gateshead, Tyne and Wear

Contents

Preface

This book contains profiles of twenty very remarkable people. Five came from Britain, four from America, two from France, and one each from Austria, Canada, Germany, Hungary, India, Ireland, Italy, the Netherlands and Spain. One was king of Spain, another president of the United States. Three were artists, three were musicians and three were writers; there were two philosophers and one philanthropist. The others were scientists: three physicists, two mathematicians and one biologist. At first sight all these people seem to have little in common except for strange idiosyncrasies, of the kind associated with the mild form of autism known as Asperger's syndrome (AS for short). As the psychologist Rosemary Dinnage has said, perhaps the current interest in the syndrome springs from some withdrawn but unrecognised streak in all of us.

Hans Asperger, a Viennese paediatrician, thought that for highly intelligent people a trace of autism could be essential to success in the arts and sciences. He believed that the typical Asperger traits of perseverance, drive for perfection, good concrete intelligence, ability to disregard social conventions and unconcern about the opinions of others could all be seen as advantageous, possibly a prerequisite for certain kinds of new thinking and creativity. Those who have the syndrome often feel as if they are on the wrong planet, and yet some of these 'strangers on the earth' have achieved so much. It must be emphasised that only a small minority of people with Asperger's have both the ability and the opportunity to excel.

Wherever possible I have quoted from the relevant literature. In psychiatry there are differences of opinion which hardly concern us here, although disagreement suggests the need for caution. The profiles are not meant as case studies. Readers who wish to know more will find details in the books and papers cited in the references. Among the psychologists and others who have kindly helped me in various ways, for example by suggesting possible subjects for profiles, I would particularly like to thank Simon Baron-Cohen, Michael Fitzgerald, Uta Frith, Gaie Houston, Mark Houston, Viktoria Lyons, Michel Treisman, John Tyrer and Rachel Warner.

Introduction

Autism, so far as we know, has always existed, in every period and culture. It is interesting to try to identify well-known people of the past who displayed some autistic traits. Sometimes these correspond to a disorder on the autistic spectrum, such as Asperger's syndrome, and there may be a discussion of such cases in the professional literature. In some instances there is disagreement among the experts as to what the disorder is or was involved. Setting such questions to one side, it is interesting to review the fascinating life stories of these very remarkable people, highlighting the patterns of behaviour that psychologists regard as significant, and that everyone would regard as extraordinary. In *Autism: Explaining the Enigma*, Uta Frith (2003) discusses some historical cases, such as the twelfth-century Italian Brother Juniper, one of the original followers of Saint Francis of Assisi. Challis and Dewey (1974) maintain that some of the 'blessed fools' of Old Russia may have been autistic too. Michael Fitzgerald has proposed the early English scientist Roger Bacon and several others. There must have been plenty of other cases, but the right kind of biographical information is not easy to find. The classical type of autism involves low intelligence, significant learning disabilities, memory by rote, literalness and a rigid insistence on sameness. However, autism is a spectrum of disorders of development, only some of which are so disabling as to make normal life impossible. The psychological, emotional and cognitive characteristics have been shown to have a biological basis, even if that is not yet well understood. The disorder has strong genetic roots. At least a third of parents of children with Asperger's syndrome will have at least some related symptoms.

Asperger's syndrome is much more common than classical autism. It is estimated to affect about one in every three or four hundred of the general population. More than half a million people in the United Kingdom have some kind of disorder on the autistic spectrum, with over 200,000 of them having Asperger's syndrome. Disorders of the autistic spectrum are found much more often in men than in women, although this may be because women are better at compensating for some of their more noticeable features, being better at social relationships and less likely to exhibit narrow interest patterns. People with the hallmarks of Asperger's syndrome may read about the symptoms and typical features and realise that these correspond to their own patterns of behaviour. Spouses may realise that their partner has the syndrome; parents that their child may have it. Teachers find cases in their pupils, not just occasionally, but quite frequently. Although the syndrome is generally considered to be a mild form of autism, it is by no means mild in its effects. I hope that those who suffer from it may derive some encouragement by reading about some of the very remarkable people who have shared some of their problems.

The syndrome was first recognised about sixty years ago, when Hans Asperger (1944) reported that some of his patients had a particular style of communication and an impairment of social adaptation, including lack of empathy, abnormality of gaze, poverty of expression and gesture, eccentricity and lack of humour. He also emphasised the sensitivity and idiosyncratic interests. At almost the same time the American psychiatrist Leo Kanner (1943) was reporting similar observations. Later the condition was formally recognised, made more specific and named Asperger's (or Asperger) syndrome, although it turned out that both Asperger and Kanner had been anticipated by the Russian neurologist G.E. Ssucharewa (1926). Over the years clinicians and researchers have proposed various diagnostic criteria, all rather similar. Because of their wonderful variety, a complete list of even the more common traits of behaviour associated with the syndrome would take up an inordinate amount of space; a useful list of over a hundred has been compiled by Norm Ledgin (2000), and that is by no means exhaustive.

The reader will find an abundance of vivid examples of these in the profiles which follow. Also the majority are collected together in the Conclusion under six headings: social impairments, all-absorbing narrow interests, repetitive routines, speech and language peculiarities, non-verbal communication problems, and motor clumsiness. Not all the patterns of behaviour associated with the syndrome, including some of the most striking, fall naturally under these headings, but most of them do. In this way the reader will, I hope, acquire a better picture of these patterns of behaviour than can be obtained from general descriptions.

The subjects of the profiles have been chosen partly with regard to diversity. The reader will doubtless be familiar with the main features of the lives of most if not all of them. Nevertheless it seemed best to include an outline in each case, rather than simply to discuss the personality of the subject. Unfortunately, information about the childhood of the subject, which could be highly significant, is often lacking. There is also a tendency to hagiography in some cases, so that the biographical information is of questionable reliability. The syndrome occurs in all sorts of people but, as Asperger himself observed, many of them seem to be particularly drawn towards professions where mathematical ability is important, social ability less so. They are attracted to mathematics and physics, and nowadays to computer science, where the syndrome is sometimes known as Silicon Valley syndrome or disorder.

However, we must not go too far. Many psychiatrists are sceptical. The profiles are not to be regarded as case studies. In the words of the well-known neurologist Oliver Sacks (2001b), 'pathologizing genius and diagnosing historical figures has become an obsession with us'. 'It seems to me extremely unlikely', he continues, 'that Wittgenstein or Einstein were significantly autistic, as compared with Cavendish, who showed a near total incomprehension of common human behaviour, social relationships and states of mind.' Ratey and Johnson (1997) have introduced the term 'shadow syndrome' for cases where individuals display only some features of Asperger's syndrome, while the economist Thomas Sowell has made a special study (2001) of very bright children who were late talkers, including the pianists Clara Schumann and Artur Rubinstein, and also the physicists Richard Feynman and Alfred Einstein.

The disorder affects different people in different ways: in each case there will be strengths and there will be weaknesses. The strengths include the ability to think in unusual and often enriching ways, and to concentrate for long periods on a single activity. Individuals with Asperger's are usually able to give their sole attention to a task and to persist with it far beyond the point at which other people would have given up. Because of their social deficit, they are usually most success-ful in areas that do not require high degrees of social understanding. The weaknesses include difficulty in understanding and using verbal and non-verbal communication, and difficulty in thinking and behaving flexibly, as well as difficulty in understanding the social world. People with Asperger's often experience an immense feeling of relief when they discover that they are not alone, that there are others who also feel they have 'arrived on the wrong planet'. Certain symptoms can be alleviated, but there is no 'cure' for it; yet some suf-ferers say that on the whole they are glad of it (for example, there is an e-mail group called AS-and-proud-of-it). In their daily lives they may feel unhappy and depressed, but there are compensations.

The psychology of most of my subjects has been considered by at least one professional, on the basis of the available information, and such expert opinions are quoted, although they do not always agree. The lay reader, however, does not need to be too concerned about the differences between various disorders on the autistic spectrum. For example, psychiatrists would distinguish Asperger's syndrome from another condition, known as high-functioning autism, but the differ-ence is not clear-cut. Most individuals with Asperger's have a strong desire to mix with others and be part of society, whereas people with high-functioning autism are often more content to be loners, living in 'their own world'. Many people with the syndrome do not succeed because their frustration and unhappiness at being 'different' prevents them from doing so. People with high-functioning autism, however, may not experience this frustration and unhappiness. When we look back into the past it is obviously going to be very difficult to be certain about this, and so I have not tried to make the distinction.

All but three of the subjects in this book are taken from the arts or sciences, but examples can be found in many other walks of life. Other illustrations can be found in fiction, for example in the early novel *The Luzhin Defence* by Vladimir Nabokov (1994), which is about a chess prodigy. The recent novels *The Curious Incident of the Dog in the Night-time* by Mark Haddon (2003) and *Haze* by Kathy Hoopmann (2003) give valuable insights into what life can be like for those affected. There have also been films, such as *Rainman*, and television programmes which have helped to raise the level of understanding of the disorder among members of the public.

There are a number of excellent books about the syndrome, some by individuals who either have it or are close to someone who does, others by professionals who study it. The information available for each of my subjects inevitably leaves some questions unanswered. It may seem surprising that biographers do not concern themselves with questions of whether the subject may have Asperger's, but autism only became clinically recognised quite recently. The biographer may describe many of the patterns of behaviour as peculiarities of the subject rather than as characteristics of a condition that affects millions throughout the world.

Some people with Asperger's also develop manic-depression, and for Isaac Newton and Vincent van Gogh, amongst others, this seems to be well established. The belief that there is a close relation between creativity and manic-depression is of long standing. In *Touched with Fire* Kay Redfield Jamison (1993) discusses this relation, as do Herschman and Lieb (1998) in their *Manic Depression and Creativity*, with many examples of remarkable people who have been afflicted by the disorder. Fitzgerald believes that mild forms of autism are also conducive to creativity, and in his book *Autism and Creativity* (2004) he discusses a number of interesting cases, including the Indian mathematician Ramanujan, the Austrian philosopher Ludwig Wittgenstein, the Irish statesman Eamonn de Valera and the British politician Sir Keith Joseph, of which the first two are also profiled here.

CHAPTER ONE

Michelangelo Buonarroti (1475–1564)

No-one should think it strange that Michelangelo loved solitude, for he was deeply in love with his art, which claims a man with all his thoughts for itself alone. (Giorgio Vasari)

For much of Michelangelo's long life his Italian homeland was in a state of turmoil. French, Spanish and German armies came and went. The popes, as secular rulers, made alliances with the great powers of Europe for or against other great powers and city states, and then broke these alliances to make others. In Rome successive popes commissioned Michelangelo to adorn the Cappella Paolina and the Sistine chapel with frescoes; a Farnese pope made him chief architect of St Peter's and entrusted him with the completion of the Farnese palace. In Florence the Medici commissioned him to execute their funerary chapel and to design the facade of San Lorenzo. Under these and other patrons Michelangelo spent his time and energy first on one project, then another; some of them were left unfinished, others have been subsequently lost. Against a background of turmoil, Michelangelo was creating immortal works of art in a life which lasted nearly ninety years. Celebrated as an architect, painter and poet, but above all as a sculptor, Michelangelo was the supreme artist.

Michelangelo's birthplace was the small Tuscan town of Caprese, near Arezzo, where his father was temporarily *podesta* (magistrate). Born on 6 March 1475 into a minor noble family, he was the second of five children, all of them boys. His father, Lodivico di Leonardo Buonarroti Simoni, was an anxious, touchy man, harsh and officious in character. As a baby Michelangelo, according to custom, was reared by a wet nurse. Significantly she was both the daughter of one stonecutter and married to another. In 1478 the Buonarrotis returned to the family villa in Settignano, just outside Florence.

When Michelangelo was six, his mother Francesca died and subsequently his father remarried. The child grew into an alert, sensitive, intelligent, introspective and quick-tempered boy. A lack of affection, due to the harshness of his father and the loss of his mother, intensified an innate shyness and reserve. A melancholy and impressionable nature left him highly vulnerable, and encouraged the habit of dealing silently with his inner struggles. When he was seven, his father, recognising his intelligence, sent him to a grammar school in Florence, where he became close to one Francesco Granacci, who shared his interest in art. Already fascinated by drawing, the boy neglected his schoolwork, for which he was scolded and beaten unreasonably by his spiteful father, who regarded art as an occupation beneath the family dignity. Eventually his father yielded and apprenticed his son at the age of fourteen to the atelier of the fresco painter Domenico Ghirlandaio, where his friend Granacci was already working. Michelangelo quickly gained the artistic skills normally acquired only after long experience.

The de facto ruler of Florence, Lorenzo de' Medici, known as the Magnificent, had established a school of sculpture in the garden of his palace on the piazza di San Marco, which was like an open-air museum of antique sculptures. Lorenzo sought out young men who wished to be trained as sculptors. Among these was Michelangelo, whose promise was so exceptional that he was invited to live in the Medici palace, which was full of antiques and decorated with beautiful paintings. There he came into contact with the circle of poets and humanists who frequented the court. Another of the young sculptors resident was Pietro Torrigiano, who described how they 'used to go into the church of the Carmine, to learn drawing from the chapel of Masaccio'. According to Torrigiano, 'It was Buonarroti's habit to banter all who were drawing there, and one day, when he was annoying me, I got more angry than usual and, clenching my fist, I gave him such a blow on the nose that I felt bone and cartilage collapse like biscuit beneath my knuckles, and this mark of mine he will carry with him to the grave.' Torrigiano was banished from Florence as a result.

After the death of Lorenzo de' Medici in 1492, Michelangelo went back to live with his father at the family villa in Settignano. Lorenzo's successor, the reckless and arrogant Piero de' Medici, often used to send for the young man and give him various minor commissions; once, when there had been a heavy fall of snow, Piero got him to make a snowman, said to have been very beautiful. Before long the incompetence of Piero's government was such that the Medici were driven out of Florence. Michelangelo thought it expedient to leave as well, so he retreated first to Venice and then to Bologna. At the end of the year, he returned to Florence, which had now become a republic. Next he moved to Rome, where he sought commissions from the Pope, Alexander Borgia, and his cardinals. The most famous of these works was the ecstatic Pietá, now in St Peter's basilica, which made his reputation as a sculptor.

Still in his mid-twenties, Michelangelo returned to Florence in 1501 and set out to consolidate the reputation he had made in Rome. The major sculpture of the next few years was the famous giant statue of David, but there were other important works (now lost), one of which was a huge mural painting that was never completed. Michelangelo was then summoned back to Rome by the formidable Julius II, who had succeeded Alexander Borgia as Pope. Julius wanted a grandiose memorial for himself, to be situated in St Peter's. He approved of the ambitious plan Michelangelo produced, and work began on its construction; however, it was only partially completed when there was a famous quarrel between sculptor and patron. Later the two men were reconciled, but even thirty years later the monument, after major changes of design, was still incomplete. Michelangelo's next major commission in the Vatican was to fresco the ceiling of the Sistine chapel, a colossal project which confirmed his reputation as a painter. When this was finished he returned to Florence where in the Medici church of San Lorenzo he created the new sacristy, with its famous sculptures, and the adjacent library. He also started work on another project to complete the facade of the church that was never carried out. In the last thirty years of his life Michelangelo concentrated his energies more on these types of architectural project. In Rome itself, the most notable were the Campidoglio, the Farnese palace, and the design of the great dome for the new basilica of St Peter's. He was also commissioned to paint the Last Judgement on the wall behind the altar of the Sistine chapel.

There is not room here to say much more about Michelangelo's many achievements, which in any case are so well known as to make this hardly necessary. During the 1540s he grew steadily more depressed and wrote to his father: 'I lead a miserable existence and reck not of life or of honour – that is of this world; I live wearied by stupendous labours and beset by a thousand anxieties. And thus I have lived for some fifteen years now and never an hour's happiness have I had.' His health had been reasonably good, apart from physical ailments including gout, renal stones and renal colic. It has been suggested that he might have suffered from goitre, which was prevalent in northern Italy due to iodine deficiency in the soil (Bondeson and Bondeson 2003). In the summer of 1544 and in December 1545 he had been seriously ill. When he was almost ninety he developed a slow fever and died on 17 February 1564. He was buried with other famous Florentines in the church of Santa Croce.

Biography in the modern sense did not arrive until the Age of the Enlightenment, but we are fortunate to have a memoir ostensibly by Michelangelo's biographer, friend and pupil Asciano Condivi. This was incorporated by Giorgio Vasari into the second edition of his celebrated *Lives of the Artists*, complementing and correcting what he had written about Michelangelo in the first edition. Condivi gives a detailed description of the artist's appearance in old age:

> Michelangelo has a good physical constitution; of body rather sinuous and bony rather than fleshy and fat; above all healthy by nature and because of his bodily exercise and his self-restraint in both sexual intercourse and in eating, although as a child he was

sickly. He always has good colour in his face; his stature is as follows: he is rather short in height, broad in the shoulders, and the rest of his body proportionate to them, though rather spare than otherwise. The form of that part of the head that is seen from the front is of a rounded figure, in such a manner that above the ears it makes a sixth part more than half a circle and thus the temples project somewhat more than the ears and the ears more than the cheeks, and these more than the rest, so that the head in proportion to the face cannot be called anything but large. The forehead in this view is square, the nose a little flattened though not by nature, for when he was a lad, one Torrigiano de Torrigiani, a bestial and proud man, almost crushed the cartilage of his nose with a blow so that he was carried home for dead...and so Michelangelo's nose, such as it is, is proportionate to the forehead and the rest of the face. The lips are thin, but the lower one somewhat fuller, so that when seen in profile it projects a little. The chin agrees well with the aforesaid parts. The forehead when seen in profile almost projects beyond the nose, and this would appear practically broken were it not for a little hump in the middle. The eyelids have few hairs; the eyes might be called small rather than otherwise but variegated and marked with yellow and blue specks. The ears are well proportioned; the hair is black and so is the beard, except that in this seventy-ninth year of his life, the hairs are copiously streaked with white; moreover the beard is four to five fingers in length, is forked and is not very thick, as may particularly be seen from his portraits. (Beck 1975)

There are so many anecdotes about Michelangelo that it is not easy to get a clear picture of his personality. Reliable biographies, such as the one by Rolf Schott (1983), help to correct the hagiography which has built up around so great an artist. Michelangelo had regular quarrels; he lost his temper easily, and would brood over any slight. Pope Leo X, who also had a fearsome temper, described him as awesome, a man to be feared. Michelangelo had major quarrels with his elderly father, who looked to him for support. According to a profile of Michelangelo at the age of forty by one of his contemporaries, 'in contradiction to so great a genius his nature was so rough and uncouth that his domestic habits were incredibly squalid and deprived posterity of any pupils who might have succeeded him. Even though he was besought by princes he would never undertake to teach anyone or even allow them to stand watching him at work' (Schott 1983). Another described him as unapproachable. Michelangelo had a way of turning rivals into enemies, real or imaginary, as happened in the case of the painter Raphael and the architect Bramante.

Michelangelo enjoyed reading Italian poetry, especially the works of Dante and Petrarch, and he wrote many madrigals and sonnets himself. Some of his poetry reflected his well-known homosexual proclivities, but most of the sonnets are addressed to the widowed Vittoria Colonna, marchioness of Pescara. When in Rome she used to hold discussions about art with kindred spirits in the beautiful convent of San Silvestro in Quirinale. Michelangelo took part in some of these discussions, and we have an account of what was said by a young Portuguese painter, Francisco de Holanda, who was present. He quotes the marchioness as saying that those who knew Michelangelo esteemed him more than his works, while those who did not know him esteemed the least part of him, which was his works. It is said that he bore her so much love that after her death he remained a long time in despair and as if out of his mind. Doubtless the account is a romanticised version of the truth, but it is said that she returned his love passionately.

Fortunately much of Michelangelo's correspondence survives. Some of it concerns the various projects on which he was engaged, but there are also numerous letters to members of the Buanarroti family. Those addressed to his self-pitying father, who looked to him for support in his old age, are often acerbic. Michelangelo had four brothers, of whom the eldest, Lionardo, became a Dominican friar, while the youngest, Sigismondo, was a simpleton who worked on the family farm. The next youngest, Giovansimone, also seems to have been simple-minded and perhaps suffered from manic-depression. That leaves the capable Buonarroto, the only brother who married; one of his progeny was an accomplished poet and playwright. Otherwise Michelangelo himself was the only member of the Buanarroti family who was at all notable. Vasari was led to comment on the contrast between the talents of Michelangelo and those of his brothers:

> the perplexity of heredity has no more striking illustration than is here to be found – brain power, nervous energy, strength of purpose, capacities of the highest quality in several directions, bestowed by nature on one son; with complete contradiction of all these qualities in the case of the other sons. (Schott 1983)

Although Michelangelo became wealthy, he led a very austere life, according to Vasari, who knew him well:

> In his youth he would be so intent on his work that he sustained himself with no more than a little bread and wine, and that was still his custom in old age. He needed little sleep; often being unable to rest, he would get up in the night and set to work with his chisel. Michelangelo rightly scorned those who injured him; but he was never known to harbour a grudge. On the contrary, he was a very patient man, modest in his behaviour and prudent and judicious in all he said. His remarks were usually profound, but he was also capable of shrewd and witty pleasantries. (Schott 1983)

Michelangelo loved and enjoyed the company of his fellow craftsmen, Vasari tells us, for whom he did countless acts of kindness. Some of these comments are plainly inconsistent with what we know from other sources; Vasari was mainly writing to please his own Medici patrons, and should not be considered a reliable source.

It is hardly surprising that the complex personality of Michelangelo has attracted the interest of psychoanalysts, from Sigmund Freud onwards, who supplement what they can learn about the external facts of his life by what they can deduce from his art. For example, the American psychiatrist Robert Liebert has written a penetrating psychoanalytic study (1983) of Michelangelo's life and images. This kind of analysis has not found favour with art historians. Other psychologists have drawn attention to the autistic traits in Michelangelo's personality, without suggesting that they provide an explanation of his genius. Most recently Arshad and Fitzgerald (2004) present the evidence for the artist having suffered from Asperger's syndrome or from high-functioning autism. They discern key features of such disorders, including poor social skills, repetitive behaviour and 'an egocentric preoccupation with unusual and circumscribed interests'. They note that he was obsessive and followed repetitive routines. His highly retentive visual memory enabled him to generate, in a remarkably short time, hundreds of sketches for the Sistine frescoes. He also had communication and conversation difficulties. He had a sarcastic wit, was bad-tempered and had outbursts of anger. At times he was paranoid, narcissistic and schizoid, Arshad and Fitzgerald add, strange, without affect and isolated. Loss of control caused him great frustration. He had no friends of any sort, and wanted none. Arshad and Fitzgerald conclude that he was preoccupied with his own private reality. Again there has been a strong reaction from those who see this as somehow detrimental to his sublime achievements.

Acknowledgment

The principal sources of information in this chapter are Arshad and Fitzgerald (2004), Beck (1975), Condivi (1976), Liebert (1983) and Schott (1983).

CHAPTER TWO

Philip of Spain
(1527–1598)

I don't know if they think I'm made of iron or stone. The truth is they need to see that I am mortal, like everyone else. (Philip II)

By any standards Philip II was one of the most remarkable men ever to sit on a throne in Europe. Although his father, the megalomaniac Habsburg emperor Charles V, had ruled vaster territories, Philip became the monarch of the greatest empire Europe had known since the Mongols and the first that encircled the globe, stretching as it did from the southern tip of Chile not only to Florida but across the Pacific to the Philippines. He ruled over a confederation of states which shared a common sovereign. The king was aided by his councils and his councillors, many of whom were of outstanding ability and efficiency, but like other absolute monarchs of the period, only he had the authority to make the decisions. Condemned to spend his days sorting out the workings of his vast web of a monarchy, he was among the few who had access to a broader perspective on its problems.

The most potent monarch of Christendom was in many ways a disaster for the unfortunate country he governed for over half a century. Until recently it was difficult to obtain a fair account of his reign. Catholic historians saw him as presiding over a Golden Age, while Protestant historians portrayed him as a fanatical Catholic, sitting like a black spider in his austere cell in the Escorial, working tirelessly day and night to crush the Dutch, to reimpose Catholicism in

England, to convert or destroy the Amerindians, and to monopolise all the riches – gold, silver, spices – of the known world. For these ends, it was said, he was prepared to imprison his own children, to assassinate opponents, and to rack and torture all who thwarted him. Neither portrayal is fair. As recent biographers have shown, Philip was far more complex and much more human than this. In the case of someone born almost five hundred years ago we can hardly expect complete certainty, but there is at least a possibility that he was affected by some disorder on the autistic spectrum, such as Asperger's syndrome, and this would help to explain some aspects of his personality which otherwise might seem puzzling.

Once Philip became king, the problems that he faced were as great as his empire. For all his power he was never in full command of events. He was unable to stop his realms being drawn into a vortex of war, debt and decay. Although he hated war and yearned for peace, he was constantly at war – not just minor wars but major wars. The immense Spanish territories in Europe were endangered on the one hand by the infidel Turks, and on the other by the heretical Flemish and the English; while France, the arch-enemy of Spain, was ready to take advantage of the situation whenever opportunities arose. Even Spain itself was never docile – regional jealousies and antagonisms were backed by centuries of tradition. The proud Spanish aristocracy were not easily tamed by either monarch or bureaucracy. Further afield the difficulty of ruling millions of Amerindians, of keeping some control over the rivalry and jealousies of his colonial governors and, at the same time, undertaking a vigorous campaign of Christianisation were as endless as they were complex.

Philip was born in the Spanish city of Valladolid on 21 May 1527, the only son of the Emperor Charles and Isabel of Portugal. When he was two, his father left Spain to join his army, then fighting the French, but continued supervising his son's upbringing from afar. In his melancholy disposition the prince took after his mother; she died when he was twelve, leaving him with two sisters, Maria and Juana. All the children of Charles V had a reputation for being curiously cold towards other people; they preferred to be alone. Later they each took meals separately even when living under the same roof. Mary was closer to her brother than Juana, who was renowned for her coldness. The lack of a loving childhood was not unusual for the sons of royalty. Everything suggests that Philip was not much interested in women. He had become adept at concealing his feelings and constraining his emotions from an early age. If he felt lust at all strongly, he appears to have kept it under strict control. Although married four times, he never seems to have been at ease with any member of the opposite sex.

His first three marriages were arranged by his father to further his political aims. The first was with his cousin Maria Manuela, princess of Portugal. In 1543 Charles had left for Germany, leaving Philip in charge as regent; he was to be away fourteen years, but continued to take a close interest in what his adolescent son was doing and retained for himself the ultimate right to make decisions. He also took a close interest in Philip's sex life, placing his daughter-in-law in the care of relatives, who had strict orders to keep her away from the prince 'except for the times which his life and health can stand', although warning his son not to use this as an excuse to consort with other women. Philip was told to remember that he was not marrying to enjoy sex, but to produce heirs. Within a few months, however, he was being reproached by both his father and his parents-in-law for treating Maria coldly.

Influenced by what he saw in the Netherlands, in 1548 his father had introduced the elaborate Burgundian ceremonial at the Spanish court. Before long the royal household had grown so large that it became impracticable to move it around whenever the king travelled. A permanent seat was needed; Philip chose the small town of Madrid, in preference to the cities of Seville or Toledo, because of its excellent water supply and room for expansion. The same year he left Spain for the first time. He sailed to Italy and, after six months there, travelled through Germany to join his father in the Netherlands. The experience made a great impression on the young prince.

In 1545 Maria had died after giving birth to a son, the unpredictable and unlovable Don Carlos. Nine years later, Philip married again. This time Charles chose his second cousin Mary Tudor, who was about to succeed to the throne of England. Mary was strongly pro-Catholic and her reign became notorious for the persecution of Protestants. Philip approved of this, although he abstained scrupulously from interfering in her affairs. He spent little over a year in England before leaving Mary and returning to the Continent to join his father, who was preparing to abdicate in his favour before retiring to spend the last years of his life in meditation at the monastery of Yuste. He handed over power in stages, but by 1556 Philip had become ruler of all his father's dominions. One of his first acts was to commission a detailed survey of the whole Iberian peninsula.

In Spain itself there were many problems to be faced. Most of all Philip dreaded the possibility that heresy might take hold in Spain as it had in the Netherlands. The basis for his attitude was not only religious but constitutional. Protestantism for Philip meant disintegration and rebellion: Catholicism meant unity and order. The repressive powers of the Inquisition, however ruthlessly employed, received his unqualified support. Compared with the rest of Europe, even Italy, Spain was remarkably free from heresy, but at the expense of shutting down the country's intellectual life. The Inquisition operated a vast network of spies and informers. Philip enjoyed watching *autos-da-fe*, the complex ritual of sentencing its victims before handing them over to the civil power for punishment, although he never stayed to watch the sentences being carried out.

When Mary died in 1558 Philip's third marriage was arranged, again by his father, and formalised early in 1560. His bride, Elisabeth de Valois, was a vivacious fourteen-year-old, twenty years his junior. It was reported that, in the early years of her marriage, she would lie awake at night hoping in vain for a visit from the king. At other times he was said to have come to her room very late, after she had fallen asleep, and then crept away again feeling virtuous at having done his duty. After two miscarriages she gave birth to a daughter, Isabella, in 1566 and then another, Catalina Micaela, the next year, but a few weeks later, when pregnant again, she became ill and died towards the end of 1568.

The Spanish royal family was no stranger to mental instability. Philip's mad grandmother Juana had been imprisoned in a windowless cell for forty years, after being forced to abdicate in her son's favour in 1517. To create alliances through marriage was a Habsburg policy and the pool of eligible royals was quite limited. As the result of inbreeding the unfortunate infante Don Carlos could only count four great-grandparents, instead of the normal eight. By 1568 it was obvious that he was becoming insane, and quite unfit to be regarded as heir to the throne. Philip decided to imprison his son, who reacted by starving himself to death.

Philip's fourth and last wife was Anna of Austria, at once his niece and daughter of his first cousin. Twenty-two years his junior, she was petite and elegant with a pale complexion, deep-blue eyes and flowing hair. He fell in love with her and she rapidly provided a male heir, Fernando. Only with Anna was there a real family life. Fernando died in 1577, but the next year Anna gave birth to another son, the future Philip III, who proved to be an imbecile. She was well into another pregnancy when she succumbed to an epidemic of influenza. The loss was to mark Philip personally; he never married again.

The triumphs and disasters of the last thirty years of Philip's reign are momentous historical events, but in the space available I can hardly do more than mention a few of them before going on to discuss the king's character and complex personality. In 1567 Philip made the fateful decision to impose his will on Flanders, where he regarded the Protestants as in rebellion against him. He sent out the Duke of Alba to deal with this, but Alba's campaign of repression only strengthened the determination of the Flemings to end Spanish rule. Elsewhere he was more successful. In 1571 the great naval victory over the Turks at Lepanto was a turning point in the long struggle to control the Mediterranean. In 1580 Philip invaded Portugal, in a successful bid for the Portuguese throne, with its vast overseas possessions. He established his court in Lisbon for a time, and even seems to have considered making the city the capital for the whole Iberian peninsula. Finally there was the disastrous expedition to invade England, with the aim of deposing Queen Elizabeth I and reimposing Catholicism in England. In 1588 the Great Armada, sent to protect the expeditionary force on its Channel crossing, was defeated by the Royal Navy and driven into the North Sea, after which it suffered many casualties as it fled back to Spain round the north of Scotland. This further failure left him deeply depressed.

Philip's administrative style was highly authoritarian. In his prime he had an enormous capacity for storing information. He required complete truthfulness from his ministers, and they were expected to respect confidentiality. However, he often kept information to himself, or told them only part of what he knew. They gave him advice but he made the decisions, even in minor matters, and once he had done so it was difficult to persuade him to think again. In the closing years of his life he displayed an almost reptilian composure. He hardly batted an eyelid when he first received news of the disaster which had befallen the Great Armada.

Philip's diet, mainly meat, remained much the same throughout his life. He obtained papal dispensation from the obligation to fast, on the grounds that a change of routine might endanger his health. He suffered greatly from gout throughout the latter part of his life, which might have been caused by the unhealthy diet he followed. He also suffered from liver cirrhosis and recurrent fevers which might have been due to malaria. After the age of sixty his health steadily declined, and eventually he was confined to an invalid carriage of his own design.

Philip was a major patron of the arts. He could play the viol and the vihuela (a sort of lute) himself, and employed a large number of court musicians. He collected Flemish paintings, for example works of Pieter Breughel and Hieronymus Bosch, and commissioned a number of paintings from Titian. He preferred the Venetian painter to El Greco, who was already in Spain, and tried to persuade Titian to come and work for him. In portraits Philip is generally shown dressed in black, as if in mourning. He formed fine collections of tapestries and silverware as well as paintings. He was a great reader, who possessed the largest private library in the Western world. Although no good at arithmetic himself, he was keen to encourage others to study it – he founded an academy of mathematics in Madrid and wished to do the same in other Spanish cities. He was imbued with an intense intellectual curiosity – the animals of the New World intrigued him, and he set up one of the first royal zoos.

Letters reveal his distinctive literary style and his extraordinary handwriting, an almost indecipherable loopy scrawl, although sometimes he could write quite legibly. When reading papers he would correct minor errors of fact, syntax or grammar. His whole day was geared to the routine of administration. After waking up, usually at 8 a.m., he read papers in bed for an hour or so. Then he rose, went to chapel, and saw officials until lunch at noon. The main business of the day began after lunch and continued until dinner at 9 p.m., often later. The royal bureaucrat had an amazing capacity for dealing with paperwork. Eminently efficient and practical, he struggled always with the immediate and the possible. He enjoyed recreations such as hunting and jousting, but the daily routine left little time for pleasure.

When Philip was twenty-eight a Scottish observer gave this description of him:

> of visage he is well favoured with a broad forehead and grey eyes, straight nosed and manly countenance. From the forehead to the point of his chin, his face groweth small; his pace is princely, and gait so straight and upright he loseth no inch of height. Philip could be tongue-tied even with intimates and when he spoke it

was in such a low voice that even those very close to him could hardly hear what he said... He always preferred to do business in writing. Throughout his life he always looked sickly – fair hair and pale skin gave him an almost albino colouring. He was fascinated with the state of his health and made a fetish of personal hygiene. He could not tolerate a single mark on the walls and floors of his rooms. The royal gaze was said to be so penetrating as to be quite disconcerting. He was aware that this made others uneasy, and usually avoided looking at petitioners, so as not to confuse them. The king's reserve was natural, not affected. Although he was uniformly courteous to his colleagues and subordinates he never exuded warmth. (Parker 1979)

In spite of two attempts on his life he never bothered with bodyguards and liked to mix freely with his subjects, usually incognito: disregard for personal safety is another autistic trait. He was never known to laugh, although he seems to have been amused by the dwarfs, buffoons and simpletons which were a feature of the Spanish court.

Architecture was a passion with Philip. The construction of the Escorial was his greatest achievement. When the king was in residence in the huge palace-monastery he would reprove the monks if they did not place the altar ornaments correctly, put out the wrong altar frontal or opened the church late. However, the construction of the Escorial was only one of his many projects. Philip also was busy remodelling other royal residences in the Flemish style. He wanted to supervise every detail of the operations. When the person in charge wrote 'I am sorry to trouble your majesty about such trifling matters', he replied: 'They do not trouble me, they delight me.' He moved incessantly from one building site to another. So regular and predictable were his movements that someone wrote a little book called *The Great and Notable Voyages of King Philip*, which began 'from Madrid to the Escorial, from the Escorial to the Pardo, from the Pardo to Aranjuez, from Aranjuez to Madrid, from Madrid to the Escorial...' Philip liked to live relatively simply, and often left most of his retinue behind when he travelled.

Philip was known as the prudent king. Suspicion, disbelief and doubt were the basis of his prudence, especially suspicion. He refused to allow a history of his reign to be written in his lifetime, and although much has been published since, our knowledge of his personality is quite limited. Even so there are indications that he may have suffered from a disorder on the autistic spectrum, and that would shed fresh light on some aspects of his character. His medical history has been described in detail by Oliveros de Castro and Subiza Martin (1956). They emphasise his solitary tendencies, his impenetrable mask of coldness, his excess of perfectionism and his inflexibility. They conclude that his personality is that of an autistic or schizotypical person, with an interior life which is difficult to interpret.

Acknowledgment

The principal sources of information in this chapter are Kamen (1997), Oliveros de Castro and Subiza Martin (1956) and Parker (1979, 1998).

CHAPTER THREE

Isaac Newton
(1642–1727)

A mind forever voyaging through strange seas of thought alone.
(William Wordsworth)

Much has been written about the complex personality of Isaac
Newton. Oliver Sacks (2001a) writes: 'Newton's emotional singularities, his jealousy and his suspiciousness, his enmities and rivalries
suggest a profound neurosis.' We have lengthy discussions of his personality by Sula Wolff (1995), Milo Keynes (1995) and Anthony Storr
(1985). Herschman and Lieb (1998) argue persuasively that he
suffered from manic-depression, while Fitzgerald (1999a) and Simon
Baron-Cohen (in James 2003b) discuss the evidence for some form of
autism, possibly Asperger's syndrome. It seems likely that Newton
suffered from both disorders. It has also been suggested that he
poisoned himself with mercury used in alchemical experiments, but if
so his health was not permanently affected.

Newton was born on 25 December 1642 in Woolsthorpe Manor, a
farmhouse near the Lincolnshire village of Colsterworth, sixty miles
north-west of Cambridge. He was premature, and at first not expected
to survive. His yeoman father, of the same name, who had only
recently married, had died three months previously. In 1645 his
widowed mother Hanna (née Aysgough) married the Reverend
Barnabas Smith, an elderly clergyman with whom she went to live in
his rectory in the nearby village of North Witham, leaving her

three-year-old son in the charge of his maternal grandparents. The boy appears to have had little affection for his grandparents, his stepfather, or the children of his mother's second marriage, and grew up as a loner.

As a youngster Newton experienced an attack of rage; these were to plague him for the rest of his years. He described it later as 'threatening my father and mother Smith to burne them and the house over them'. He also recorded 'striking many', 'peevishness with my mother', 'punching my sister' and 'falling out with the servants' (White 1997). While he was evidently a trial to the household, a woman who knew him during these years recalled him as a 'sober silent thinking lad, and was never known scarce to play with the boys abroad, at their silly amusements, but would rather choose to be at home, even among the girls' (Stukeley 1936), his half-sisters. He spent his time in building working models of mills and other simple machines.

At the age of twelve, after early education at local schools, Newton was sent to King's School at the market town of Grantham. During school terms he lodged with an apothecary named Clark, who seems to have treated him kindly and, in particular, encouraged him to go on making things with his hands. On the death of her second husband in 1656, his mother returned to Woolsthorpe with three children from her second marriage. Two years later she took the fourteen-year-old Isaac away from school to help her manage the family farm. He proved a somewhat incompetent farmer, his mind too much on other things. His friend and first biographer the antiquarian William Stukeley (1936) relates:

> On going home from Grantham, 'tis usual at the town end to lead a horse up Spittlegate Hill, being very steep. Sir Isaac had been so intent in his meditations that he never thought of remounting at the top of the hill and so had led his horse home all the way, being five miles…the horse by chance slipt his bridle and went home but Sir Newton walked on with the bridle in his hand, never missing the horse.

On the advice of a maternal uncle, Newton was sent back to school to prepare for entry to the University of Cambridge. He was nineteen. He was admitted to Trinity College where he settled down to a hardworking, abstemious existence, buried in his studies. The notebooks he kept in those years document his feelings of sadness, anxiety, fear and low self-esteem. The only friend he made among his fellow students described Newton as being solitary and dejected. In 1662 the young man experienced a depressive crisis that took the form of an obsession with sins, real and imaginary. He listed all the transgressions he could remember committing from his childhood onwards, some of which we have quoted. Problems with rage and suicidal thought are suggested by one cryptic entry: '…wishing deathe and hoping it for some'. In 1664 he had a breakdown caused, he believed, by overwork and staying up late to observe a comet.

During the Great Plague of 1665–66 the Cambridge colleges were suspended and so Newton went home to Woolsthorpe. It was then that he made the revolutionary discoveries in mathematics and physics that formed the foundation for much of his own subsequent work, and affected the future course of science. Above all he conceived the theory of universal gravitation and the new cosmology based on it. When asked how he did so, Newton said, 'It was through concentration and sheer dedication. I keep the subject constantly before me, till the first dawnings opens slowly, little by little and little into the full and clear light.' Looking back on his achievements at an advanced age, Newton said, 'All this was in the two plague years of 1665 and 1666 for in those days I was in the prime of my age for invention and minded mathematics and philosophy more than any time since.'

In 1667, after the university reopened, Newton's abilities were starting to be recognised. Trinity elected him to a minor fellowship, against strong competition, and when this was converted into a major fellowship the following year he was entitled to reside in the college indefinitely. He acquired a patron in Isaac Barrow, the first Lucasian professor of mathematics, who vacated his chair in Newton's favour after a few years. Newton first lectured as Lucasian professor in January 1670. The subject was optics: the audience was small and no one attended the second lecture. He continued addressing an empty room throughout every lecture he gave for the next seventeen years, after which he gave up all pretence at teaching.

His assistant and amanuensis Humphrey Newton (no relation) recalled: 'I never knew him to take any recreation or pastime either in riding out to take the air, walking or bowling or any other exercise whatever, thinking all hours lost that was not spent in his studies, to which he kept so close that he seldom left his chamber.' On the rare occasions when Newton was in the company of others he contributed little to conversations. Humphrey recalled, 'He would with great acuteness answer a question, but would never start one.' During the five years they were together Humphrey only knew Newton laugh once, and that was when someone asked him what was the use of studying Euclid, 'upon which Sir Isaac was very merry'.

Newton's early enthusiasm for making working models had developed into a passion for making scientific apparatus, especially optical instruments. The celebrated reflecting telescope was a notable example of his remarkable skill and manual dexterity. It was this that first brought him to the attention of the members of the Royal Society of London, who asked to see it. Newton sent them an improved model, which was received with acclamation. When he followed this up with a paper about his optical research, he was elected to the society forthwith. It was in 1670, or thereabouts, that Newton first developed an interest in alchemy, which began as an offshoot of chemical experiments but soon developed into an obsession. He studied the literature exhaustively and made contact with other enthusiasts. He was also fascinated by biblical chronology and numerology. The mass of writings Newton left on esoteric and theological matters has left most scholars perplexed, but F.E. Manuel (1963) and others have re-examined this material and thrown fresh light on its significance.

Humphrey gave a description of his master's routine at this time:

> He rarely went to bed till 2 or 3 of the clock, sometimes not until 5 or 6, lying [in bed] about four of five hours, especially at spring or fall of leaves, at which times he used to employ about 6 weeks in his elaboratory, the fire scarcely going out either night or day; he sitting up one night as I did another, till he had finished his chemical experiments, in the performance of which he was the most accurate, strict, exact. What his aim might be I was not able to penetrate, but his pains, his diligence made me think he aimed at something beyond the reach of human art and industry.

Humphrey continued:

> So intent, so serious upon his studies that he ate very sparingly, nay, at times he has forgot to eat at all, so that, going in to his chamber, I have found his mess untouched, of which, when I have reminded him, he would reply – have I? – and then making to the table, would take a bite or two standing, for I cannot say I ever saw him sit at table by himself.

He added:

> Newton's forgetfulness of his dinner was an excellent thing for his old housekeeper, who sometimes found both dinner and supper scarcely tasted of, which the old woman has very pleasantly and mumpingly gone away with. On getting out of bed in the morning, he has been discovered to sit at his bedside for hours without dressing himself, utterly absorbed in thought. (Manuel 1963)

Even in his later years, if he was working on something that interested him, Newton would not pause to eat until he had worked through the night:

> When he sometimes took a turn or two [in his garden for a walk]
> he has made a sudden stand, turn'd himself about, run up ye
> stairs like another Archimedes, with an eureka, fall to write on
> his desk standing, without giving himself the leisure to draw a
> chair to sit down on... At some seldom times when he designed
> to dine in ye hall, he would turn to the left hand and go out into
> the street, when making a stop when he found his mistake,
> would hastily turn back and then sometimes instead of going
> into ye hall, would return to his chamber again. (Manuel 1963)

Newton often failed to notice he had missed a meal. Even if he reached
the dining hall, he might sit down, lost in thought, while the courses
came and went without him noticing them. Sometimes Newton
invited people to his rooms for a glass of wine, but if an idea came to
him while he was fetching wine from another room, he would sit
down to work on it, completely forgetting the guests who were
waiting for him.

In 1684 Newton's friend, the astronomer Edmund Halley, came to
visit him in Cambridge, and this marked a turning point in his scientific career. Almost twenty years had elapsed since Newton had conceived of the universal law of gravitation, and still he had not written
an account of his new cosmology. Spurred on by repeated exhorta-
tions from Halley he composed the *Principia* between the autumn of
1684 and the spring of 1686; it appeared the following year under its
full title *Philosophiae Naturalis Principia Mathematicae*. The work transformed Newton from a physicist and mathematician known to only a
few fellow-scientists into an international celebrity. The great French
scientist Pierre-Simon Laplace wrote: 'The *Principia* is pre-eminent
above any other production of the human genius.' In spite of the
success of the *Principia* and of his later *Opticks*, Newton remained publication shy. 'I need not what there is desirable in public esteem, were I
able to acquire or maintain it,' he said. 'It would perhaps increase my
acquaintance, the thing which I chiefly study to decline.' This reluc-
tance to publish led to some of his most notorious priority disputes,
notably with his compatriot Robert Hooke and with the German
Gottfried Leibniz.

By 1687 Newton was considering giving up scientific work. He wrote to a fellow-scientist:

> I see I have made myself a slave to philosophy [science], but...I will resolutely bid adieu to it eternally, excepting what I do to my private satisfaction, or leave it to come out after me [after his death] for I see a man must either resolve to put out nothing new, or become a slave to defend it. (Gleick 2003)

He tried to exchange his professorship of mathematics for one of law, and was interested in the idea of becoming provost [head] of King's, another major Cambridge college. He served as a member of parliament for one year, and made some new friends in the capital. At the same time he became obsessed with the pseudoscience of alchemy, and began writing a treatise on the subject.

It was about this time that the young Swiss mathematician Fatio de Duillier entered his life. Fatio seems to have won his way into Newton's affections like no one else. Twenty-two years younger than Newton, Fatio had studied science in Paris. Although not without talent, he showed an early flair for self-promotion, and soon after arriving in London in 1687 was elected to the Royal Society. He acquired the nickname 'the ape [imitator] of Newton'. Although much of the correspondence between Newton and his beloved Fatio has been lost, what survives seems much more intimate than Newton's other correspondences. The relationship came to an abrupt end in the summer of 1693 when Newton's major psychotic episode began.

During this period Newton suffered confusion, memory loss, anorexia, acute insomnia, rage and paranoia. When the agitation subsided, he passed into a deep, despairing depression, in which he tried to break with all his friends, such as John Locke and Samuel Pepys. He wished Locke was dead, accusing him of designing 'to sell him an office or to embroil him with women'. In a letter to Pepys, Newton said: 'I am extremely troubled at the embroilment I am in, and have neither ate nor slept well this 12 months, nor have my former consistency of mind' (Gleick 2003). He had sufficient insight to realise that he had not been mentally normal for a year and still did not feel well. He then added that he wanted to have nothing more to do with anyone, a feeling typical of intense depression. 'I am now sensible that I must withdraw from your acquaintance and see neither you nor the rest of my friends any more, if I may but leave them quietly' (Gleick 2003).

Soon after Pepys received this disturbing letter, he wrote to a mutual friend in his anxiety about Newton's sanity:

> I had lately received a letter from him so surprising to me from the inconsistency of every part of it, as to be put in great disorder by it, from the concernment I have for him, lest it should arise from that which of all mankind I should least dread from him and most lament for, I mean a discomposure in health, or mind, or both. (Gleick 2003)

The mutual friend went to see how Newton was and reported to Pepys:

> He told me that he had writ to you a very odd letter, at which he was much concerned, added that it was in a distemper [illness] that much seized his head, and that kept him awake 5 nights together, which upon occasion he desired I would represent to you, and beg your pardon, he being very much ashamed he should be so rude to a person for whom he hath so great an honour. He is now very well, and though I fear he is under some degree of melancholy, yet I think there is no reason to suspect it hath at all touched his understanding, and I hope it never will. Gleick 2003)

Newton did not immediately recover from his 'small degree of melancholy', and five years would pass before he felt the desire to undertake another major project. Meanwhile, rumours that Newton had lost his mind began to circulate in the scientific world. The Dutch scientist Christiaan Huygens, no stranger to melancholia himself, heard that 'Isaac Newton, the celebrated mathematician, 18 months previously had become deranged in his mind'. Huygens added: 'He has lately so far recovered his health as to begin again to understand his own *Principia*.' However, Newton never recovered 'the former consistency of his mind'; it was said that 'he had something rather languid in his look and his manner'. Moreover Herschman and Lieb (1998) believe that this major crisis in Newton's life had other lasting effects:

Those who undergo the severer states of melancholia often develop grandiose delusions about their own importance, and they believe themselves to be so far above their fellow men that other human beings appear negligible to them. It is not uncommon for their delusions to have religious content, inclining them to see themselves as prophets or messiahs divinely ordained to fulfil some great mission. Newton not only developed these ideas when he was intensely ill, but for most of his life he also retained them among his beliefs about reality. He believed that legend and folklore had predicted his personal greatness. Identifying himself as the only living scientist whose work had truth or significance, he felt that the work of other scientists was either trivial, addenda to his own findings, or plagiarisms of it. In his alchemical and religious writings he indicated that he alone among his contemporaries was appointed by God to bring his truth to the world. Newton further held that everything worth knowing would be revealed to him.

For some years Newton, who was tired of academic life, had been making repeated but unsuccessful attempts to obtain a position in London. Finally, in 1696, he was appointed to the remunerative office of Warden of the Royal Mint. This enabled him to move to the capital where he was joined by his niece Catherine Barton, whose mother was one of his step-sisters and whose father had died three years previously. A witty and charming girl of seventeen, she soon became very popular in London society, the toast of the Kit-Kat club. She acted as Newton's housekeeper and helped him to develop a social life. In his memoir Stukeley (1936) wrote that Newton 'could be very agreeable in company and even sometimes talkative' at this time, and that he

> ...had in his disposition a natural pleasantness of temper, very distant from moroseness, attended neither with gaiety nor levity, and much good nature. He used a good many sayings, bordering on joke and wit. In company he behaved very agreeably courteous, affable, he was easily made to smile if not to laugh.

Previously it had been said of him that 'he was full of thought...and spoke very little in company, so that his conversation was not agreeable'.

Newton's house had become the scene of large gatherings of the intelligentsia. Foreign savants were included, as were non-scientific aristocrats to whom he offered membership of the Royal Society, although Newton had not attended meetings of the society himself. This was partly because he would have encountered the curator Robert Hooke, one of his principal adversaries. In 1703, after Hooke's death, Newton was elected president, an office to which he was re-elected annually for the rest of his life. Once in the chair he exercised complete domination over the society. However, even when president, Newton did not find it easy to express his fundamental convictions in public; he preferred silence to the risk of criticism in which he might find himself an object of ridicule. In 1705 he was knighted for his services to science during a Royal visit to Cambridge.

Newton's relationships with other people, particularly scientists, were often fraught. One friend disagreed with Newton over a biblical interpretation, and Newton refused to speak to him for a year. William Whiston, Newton's choice as successor to the Lucasian chair at Cambridge, explained:

> so did I enjoy a large portion of his favour for 20 years together. But he then perceiving that I could not do as his other darling friends did, that is learn from him, without contradicting him, when I differed in opinion from him, he could not…bear such contradiction.

He described Newton as 'of the most fearful, cautious and suspicious temperament that I ever knew'. Newton turned against his loyal friend Halley for a while because the astronomer was not, in Newton's opinion, sufficiently serious about religion. Stukeley was banished from Newton's acquaintance for trying to become secretary of the Royal Society without first asking his approval. Stukeley reported: 'Sir Isaac show'd a coolness toward me for two or three years, but as I did not alter in my carriage and respect toward him, after that he began to be friendly to me again.' While friends often found Newton difficult, enemies found him ruthless, disingenuous, unjust and cruel. In his later years he became yet more aggressive, seeming to seek out targets for his wrath.

Newton's character, like that of many of those with Asperger's syndrome, is remarkable for its opposing traits. His biographers claim that he was stingy and generous, modest and megalomaniacal, high principled and unscrupulous. He was a man of rigorous logic, an exemplar in the use of the scientific method, while simultaneously an alchemist who cherished strange delusions. His conduct was as contrasting as his moods and opinions. He raged at the prisoners who had been debasing the coinage and counterfeiting, and he showed no mercy when they were beaten and executed. Nevertheless, 'a melancholy story would often draw tears from him, and he was exceedingly shocked by any act of cruelty to man or beast, mercy to both being the topic he loved to dwell on'. John Conduitt, who married Catherine Barton and eventually succeeded Newton at the Mint, tells us that '[Newton] had a lively and piercing eye, a comely and gracious aspect, with a fine head of hair as white as silver, without any baldness, and when his peruke was off he was a venerable sight'. His grandniece, who knew him in his later years, was impressed with his love of children and thought him cheerful.

According to Stukeley, 'Sir Isaac by his great prudence and naturally good constitution, had preserved his health to old age,' although, like many who have experienced depression, he had delusions of ill-health and dosed himself for non-existent tuberculosis. In old age he became corpulent and rather deaf. When Newton lay on his deathbed, Conduitt recorded later: 'He had violent fits of pain with very short intermissions, and though drops of sweat ran down from his face with anguish, he never complained or cried out, or showed the least peevishness or impatience, and during the short intervals from that violent torture, would smile and talk with his usual cheerfulness.' At the end of his life Newton saw beyond his delusion of having been given the keys to the secrets of the universe and said, 'I do not know what I may appear to the world. But to myself I seem to have been only a boy, playing on the sea shore and diverting myself in now and then finding a smoother pebble or a prettier shell than ordinary, while the great ocean of truth lay undiscovered before me.' Newton died on 20 March 1727, at the age of eighty-five. Following a state funeral he was buried in Westminster Abbey, where his monument lies in a prominent position in the nave while clustered around his feet lie memorials to other great British scientists. In Newton, wrote David Hume, this island may boast of having 'produced the greatest and rarest genius that ever rose for the ornament and instruction of the species'.

The mathematician Augustus De Morgan, one of the first to try to understand Newton's character, wrote in 1885: '[Newton] had not within himself the resource from whence to inculcate high and true motives of action upon others. The fear of man was before his eyes. All his errors are to be traced to a disposition which seems to have been born with him.' More recently his biographer Louis Trenchard More (1934) amplified this:

> He was singularly unable to form intimate friendships. Morbidly suspicious and secretive, he was subject to peevish outbreaks of ill-temper, even towards those who were his best friends. On such occasions he stooped to regrettable acts which involved him in a succession of painful controversies that plagued his life, robbed him of the just fruits of his work, and disheartened his sincere admirers. The Gods had showered on him at birth extraordinary gifts such as have been given to almost no other man, but some evil fate cursed him with a suspicious and jealous temperament which marred his life. This taint in his blood did not show itself in the form of ordinary vanity but in an inordinate sensitiveness to any personal criticism or to a reflection on his personal honour. In spite of his love of meditation and of peace free of all distractions it involved him in constant quarrels and altercations; and during a long and illustrious life it raised an impenetrable barrier between him and other men. To his friends he was never more than lukewarm and he kept them constantly uneasy lest they had offended him; to his rivals he was, at times, disingenuous, unjust and cruel.

Acknowledgment

The principal sources of information in this chapter are De Morgan (1885), Fara (2002), Fitzgerald (1999a), Gleick (2003), Herschman and Lieb (1998), Keynes (1995), Manuel (1963), Stukeley (1936), Storr (1985), Westfall (1993) and White (1997).

CHAPTER FOUR

Jonathan Swift (1667–1745)

Swift has a natural severity of face, which even his smiles could scarcely soften, or his utmost gaiety render placid and serene. When he was angry, this natural severity becomes frightening, it is scarcely possible to imagine looks, or features, that carried with them more terror and austerity. (Lord Orrery)

Could Jonathan Swift, the author of *Gulliver's Travels* and other classics of the English language, have had Asperger's syndrome? Fitzgerald (2005) confirms that Swift satisfies most of the usual diagnostic criteria. There was his obsession with physical exercise, his preoccupation with personal cleanliness, and its extreme opposite, filth, also his fondness for making lists. Swift was a famous talker, who contrived to dominate any conversation with a blaze of politeness. He was adamant that no one should ever have power over him: 'The power to melt his self-possession, the power to hurt.' Nobody could be a warmer friend, it was said, but it was on condition that his friends should be part of himself. He annexed others rather than attracted them. Swift was a cantankerous genius, a man of intense responses, building up to towering rage. It all adds up.

Swift was born in Dublin on 30 November 1667. His father, also named Jonathan, was an impecunious lawyer who held the office of steward of the King's Inns in Dublin. His mother Abigail (née Erick) gave birth to two children; the eldest was a daughter Jane, born shortly

Dean Swift

before the sudden death of Jonathan senior. Our Jonathan's English nurse, who was very fond of him, had to return home and took the boy with her, soon after his first birthday, without telling his widowed mother. Before long his mother returned to her family in Leicester with her daughter Jane, leaving her son in Ireland with an uncle named Godwin. So he was not only fatherless, he was very largely separated from his mother as well.

A sickly child, Jonathan was mainly brought up by Godwin and other members of his late father's family. After completing his school education at Kilkenny College, at the age of fifteen he matriculated at Trinity College, Dublin. As a student he was troublesome and rebellious, often being censured for misbehaviour. He stayed on at Trinity College for a time after graduating and then went to join his mother in England, by which time he was twenty. There Swift found a patron in the able retired diplomat Sir William Temple, whose father had been a close friend of Swift's uncle Godwin. Temple installed Swift at Moor Park, his country seat in Surrey. According to the historian Macaulay, 'Little did Temple imagine that the coarse exterior of his dependant concealed a genius equally suited to politics and to letters, a genius destined to shake great kingdoms, to stir the laughter and the rage of millions, and to leave to posterity memorials which can perish only with the English language.' 'Coarse' may not be the right word, but there was something disagreeable about Swift. He was squarely and solidly built, with a high-domed forehead, a strongly curved nose, a small well-shaped mouth. His eyes were expressive, protuberant and bright blue, under bushy eyebrows.

While Swift was at Moor Park he was entrusted by Sir William with a mission that took him to London where he had an interview with the king. Characteristically he made the journey on foot, almost fifty miles each way. He now thought of going to Oxford to qualify for the degree of MA, but when he got there he changed his mind and decided instead to go to Ireland and take Holy Orders. When this was accomplished he was presented to an obscure rural parish near Belfast but soon gave it up and returned to Moor Park, where he acted as secretary to Sir William. Much of the next ten years he devoted to study, as much as ten hours a day, but every two hours he would interrupt his work to run up and down a nearby hill, about half a mile in six minutes. All his life physical exercise was an obsession with Swift, who protested continually that without his walk or ride he could not exist at all. It was during this period he wrote *The Battle of the Books* and the greater part of his first masterpiece, *A Tale of a Tub*, a celebrated prose satire on corruption in religion and learning, although these works were not published until some years later. There is also a curious list of resolutions in his hand, headed 'When I Come to be Old', that reads:

> Not to marry a young woman.
>
> Not to keep young Company unless they reelly desire it.
>
> Not to be peevish or morose, or suspicious.
>
> Not to scorn present Ways, or Wits, or Fashions, or Men, or War &c.
>
> Not to be fond of Children, or let them come near me hardly.
>
> Not to tell the same story over and over to the same People.

Not to be covetous.

Not to neglect decency or cleenlyness, for fear of falling into Nastyness.

Not to be over severe with young People, but give Allowance for their youthfull follyes and weaknesses.

Not to be influenced by, or give ear to knavish tatling Servants, or others.

Not to be too free of advise, nor trouble any but those that desire it.

...

Not to talk much, nor of my self.

Not to boast of my former beauty, or strength, or favor with Ladyes &c.

Not to hearken to Flatteryes, nor conceive that I can be beloved by a young woman.

...

Not to be positive or opinionative.

Not to sett up for observing all these Rules, for fear I should observe none.

(Swift 1897)

Swift was very fond of making lists. Perhaps this one, dated 1699, reflects his observations of Sir William in old age, but the first and fifth resolutions seem to apply more to Swift himself.

After Temple's death it was found that in his will Swift, as well as being left some money, had been appointed literary executor. Accordingly Swift edited and published Sir William's memoirs, which displeased Temple's sister, Lady Giffard, who conveyed her annoyance to influential acquaintances, causing him lasting harm. Swift needed to secure a living and decided that his chances of preferment would be better in Ireland. There, after several disappointments, he was appointed to the parish of Laracor, near the ancient town of Trim, to which was added a prebend of St Patrick's cathedral. Once installed in his living he set sail for England, the first of a series of lengthy visits over the next seven years. One of his major accomplishments in this period was the completion and publication of *A Tale of a Tub*. At the end of his life, when no longer in his perfect mind, Swift was found turning the pages of a copy and muttering, 'Good God, what a genius I had when I wrote that book.'

Lady Giffard had a companion and housekeeper named Bridget Johnson whose daughter Esther (Hetty) was to become, as Stella, the most important woman in Swift's life. Esther bore a striking likeness to Temple, whose natural child she might have been. Sir William had left Mrs Johnson some property that enabled her to leave Moor Park and settle down with her daughter at nearby Farnham. On his return to Ireland in 1701 Swift was accompanied by the daughter and her chaperone, who settled down in Dublin, while Swift went back to England. Swift had from nature a supreme gift, an irresistible charm in personal intercourse which attracted the favour and desire of women, to whom his behaviour was always a mixture of tyrannising and petting. In later years he issued annually an edict commanding all ladies to make the first advances. In the *Journal* he often mentions a Mrs Vanhomrigh, the widow of a Dutch merchant who had followed William III to Ireland and became wealthy as a result. Mrs Vanhomrigh's daughter Esther, who he called Vanessa, fell in love with him after her mother died, but Swift was unresponsive.

In 1710 Swift was made Dean of St Patrick's; the deanery became his Dublin home. He began to realize he would never rise any higher in the Church. The letters he wrote Esther from England between September 1710 and June 1713 form the famous *Journal to Stella*. They make use of the childish 'little language' that he used exclusively in conversation and correspondence with Stella; his pet name for her was Poppet, for himself Presto (Italian for swift). In them we find fascinating details about Swift's daily life in London during the closing years of Queen Anne's reign. Swift's involvement in the political pandemonium of those years culminated in his great pamphlet 'The Conduct of the Allies', condemning the ruinous war that had dragged on since 1701.

The death of Queen Anne in 1714 swept Swift's Tory friends out of office; to secure his deanery he hurried back to Ireland, his place of exile. Although hating to be called Irish, he was a zealous promoter of Irish causes in London in the years ahead. Before long he was in England again, living quietly in the rectory of an old friend at Upper Letcombe in Berkshire, trying to forget about politics. There were, however, problems in his personal affairs. Vanessa began to suspect that Swift had secretly married Stella. There was some kind of confrontation after which Vanessa complained of his 'killing words' and the 'awful look which strikes her dumb'. She died shortly afterwards. Around 1720 Swift had begun work on *Gulliver's Travels*, his second masterpiece, which was published in 1726. The book was an immediate success, and has taken its place as one of the classics of the English language.

Meanwhile Stella's health had been declining, and when she died early in 1728 Swift lost his dearest, most intimate companion. After this he never left Ireland again. 'I reckon no man is thoroughly miserable,' he said, 'unless he be condemned to live in Ireland.' He was showing increasing signs of decay. His temper became morose. He found it difficult to read because he had grown long-sighted and refused to wear spectacles. He filled his time with excessive exercise. Some of the scatological poems he published about this time show the morbid dwelling on filth that was unfortunately characteristic. Swift was remarkable for scrupulous personal cleanliness but seems to have tormented himself with what revolted him. In *Gulliver's Travels* the hero, on his return after five years, says that:

> as soon as I entered the house, my wife took me in her arms and kissed me; at which, having not been used to the touch of that odious animal for so many years, I fell in a swoon of almost an hour... I could not endure my wife or children in my presence, the very smell of them was intolerable. (Swift 1933)

All his life Swift had a poor memory that grew worse as he aged. Since early manhood he had also suffered from recurrent fits of giddiness that continued to plague him in the years ahead. The cause of this was labyrinthine vertigo, or Ménière's syndrome. The disease attacks the inner ear, causing deafness or vertigo or both. It can start at various ages, with no warning, and comes in recurrent spells that may grow more unpleasant and more extended as the victim ages. Sufferers may have violent fits of vomiting; often they feel too dizzy to stand up, and sometimes they lose their hearing. Today, as a palliative, they take daily the pills prescribed against seasickness, and usually have no further trouble.

Swift often complained of his poor memory, his deafness and his nauseous seizures, but there was worse to come. Shortly before his seventy-fifth birthday he suffered a feverish and painful inflammation of the eye socket called orbital cellulitis. He went into the sort of decline that a brain lesion associated with cerebral arterio-scelerosis can produce. He suddenly had great difficulty expressing himself or understanding others. During the last three years of his life Swift only uttered a few, rare, disconnected exclamations. His symptoms were those of motor aphasia, inability to speak, usually combined with some inability to understand speech. People in this state can often make emotional exclamations but not propositional statements. By the end of 1738 Swift was no longer fully responsible for his actions. This had nothing to do with psychosis, madness, insanity or imbecility. However, the most convenient way for a senile person, living alone, to be defended against various sorts of exploitation was for there to be a declaration of lunacy, and so Swift's friends took the necessary steps.

Jonathan Swift died on 19 October 1745, at the age of seventy-eight, and was buried at midnight in St Patrick's cathedral, alongside the grave of his beloved Stella. The epitaph he wrote for himself, translated into English, reads:

> Here lies the body of Jonathan Swift D.D. Dean of this Cathedral Church. Where wrathful indignation can tear his heart no further. Go passer-by and imitate if you can one who spent himself to the utmost in Freedom's cause. Died October 19, 1745. Aged 78.

He was a man of proud and masterful nature doomed to dependence on weaker men; suffering till past middle life from hope deferred and forced to eat his heart out in exile. He could be both humorous and playful when in good spirits with congenial society; but his humour always had a sardonic tinge, and he seldom if ever laughed. His fun was always mixed with contempt and he was incapable of pitying his victims. If his eyes were opened by personal antipathy, he saw most clearly the really bad side of his enemies; his indignation was as genuine as it was intense.

Acknowledgment

The principal sources of information in this chapter are Acworth (1947), Ehrenpreis (1958), Fitzgerald (2005), Forster (1875) and Glendinning (1988).

CHAPTER FIVE

John Howard
(c. 1726–1790)

[Howard's] way of thinking and acting was marked by a certain singularity. (John Aikin)

The social reformer John Howard was born in a place just north of London on 2 September 1726 – the year is uncertain. His father, of the same name, was a partner in an upholstery and carpet business; John Howard senior was a 'strict Protestant dissenter of a penurious disposition in whose household great order and regularity were observed'. His wife, whose maiden name was Cholmley, died when her son was five; she had an older daughter named Ann. Young Howard, a sickly child, spent his early days at the Bedfordshire village of Cardington, where his father had a small property. After seven years at a school in Bedford the boy went on to the Moorfields Dissenting Academy for three years, where he was taught by John Eames, a learned man and fellow of the Royal Society. Even so, Howard was never able to speak or write his native language without quite childish mistakes. 'In estimating the powers of his mind,' wrote his original biographer John Aikin (1792), 'it rather adds to the account, that he had this additional difficulty to combat in the pursuit of the great objective of his later years.'

After leaving school Howard was apprenticed to a London firm of wholesale grocers. His father died in 1742, leaving his son and daughter well provided for. Howard obtained a release from his indentures and, wanting to see something of the world, went on a Continental tour, the first of several. After returning to England he lived in London, studying science and medicine. At some stage he became ill and his landlady, a widow of fifty-two, took great care of him. Although less than half her age Howard married her, out of gratitude. Their married life was cut short by her death in November 1755, the year of the catastrophic Lisbon earthquake. Howard decided to go and inspect the damage it had caused, but the ship on which he was sailing there was captured by a French privateer. The crew and the passengers were carried as prisoners to France, then at war with England, where they suffered great privations. Returning to England on parole he successfully negotiated an exchange for himself, and having described to the Commissioners of Sick and Wounded Seamen the sufferings of his fellow prisoners, their release was obtained from the French government.

In May 1756 Howard was elected a fellow of the Royal Society, on the nomination of his former teacher John Eames; three of his papers were published in the *Philosophical Transactions*, one on the degree of cold observed at Cardington in the winter of 1762, one on the heat of the waters of Bath, and one on the heat in the ground of Vesuvius. Meteorological observations were much to his taste, we are informed; when the weather was frosty he used to get out of bed early every morning to read a thermometer in his garden. Even in the depth of winter he made a practice of taking cold baths, whenever possible, or failing that he would lie down, for some considerable time, between a pair of bed-sheets, damped for the express purpose of communicating to his body the right degree of coldness. Throughout his life he rose at dawn, took his cold bath, and after prayers dressed himself 'after the style of a plain Quaker'. His diet for the whole day consisted of nothing more than 'two penny rolls with some butter or sweetmeat, a pint of milk and five or six dishes of tea with a roasted apple before going to bed'.

Cardington was a poor sort of village but Howard believed it could be improved, and he made it his principal home for the rest of his life. In 1758 he married Henrietta Leeds, daughter of a Cambridgeshire serjeant-at-law. Unlike his first wife she was close to him in age, and she shared his interest in improving the Cardington estate. Prior to his second marriage Howard appears to have made an agreement with Henrietta 'that to prevent altercations about those little matters which he had observed to be the chief grounds of uneasiness in families, he should always decide' (Aikin 1792). He now busied himself in erecting model cottages on his Cardington property; the tenants of these were required to attend Divine Service regularly and avoid the ale-house. The sick, the disabled and the aged were objects of his charity. He also provided for the elementary education of the village children. The girls were taught reading and needlework, the boys reading, writing and arithmetic.

When Henrietta decided that the Bedfordshire climate did not agree with her, they moved to a house near Lymington, in the New Forest, where they lived for two or three years. Eventually they returned to Cardington where, after seven years of marriage, they had a child, a son also named John. Henrietta died four days after he was born. In the following year, being again in poor health, Howard took the cure at Bath. When he recovered he made a short excursion through Holland, and two years later he made a longer tour, visiting France, Switzerland, Holland, Italy and Germany. In these early travels he acquired or strengthened a taste in the fine arts, and obtained paintings and other works of art with which he embellished his seat at Cardington. After returning from the Continent he spent some time touring Wales and southern Ireland. This was followed by another lengthy period of ill-health.

In Howard's day the highest civil office in a county was that of High Sheriff. The holder was nominally responsible for many things, including the safe custody of criminals and those awaiting trial. Although Howard was a dissenter he was unable to avoid being appointed High Sheriff of Bedfordshire in 1773, and this led directly to his life's work as a prison reformer. In his official capacity the defective arrangements of the prisons and the intolerable distress of the prisoners were brought immediately under his notice. He was shocked at discovering that people could be confined in jail until certain fees were paid to the jailer even if they had been declared not guilty. Howard proposed to the Bedfordshire justices that the jailer should be paid a salary in lieu of fees. The justices replied by asking for a precedent for charging the county with the expense. Howard accordingly rode into the neighbouring counties in order to find one, but failed to discover a single case in which a jailer was paid a fixed salary. He went on examining the houses of correction, the city and county jails, throughout the land, paying particular attention to sickness among prisoners due to infections such as typhus and smallpox.

In March 1774 Howard gave evidence before the House of Commons in committee, and was afterwards called to the bar to receive the thanks of the House 'for the humanity and zeal which have led him to visit the several jails of this kingdom, and to communicate to the House the interesting observations he has made on the subject'. Subsequently two bills were passed, one for the abolition of jailer's fees and the other for improving the sanitary state of prisons and the better preservation of the health of prisoners. Though copies of these Acts were printed at Howard's expense and sent by him to the keeper of every county jail in England, their provisions were for the most part evaded.

When Howard stood for Parliament in 1774, he was narrowly defeated. Meanwhile he continued his self-imposed task of inspecting prisons and, after returning from a visit to Scotland and Ireland in the spring of 1775, set off for France. In Paris he visited the principal prisons but failed to gain access to the Bastille. From France he went on a tour of inspection through Holland, Flanders and Germany, and returned to England in July. A few months later he set out on another general inspection of the English jails. Two years later his report *The State of the Prisons* was published, and made him an instant celebrity. The appalling abuses that were exposed in it gave the first impetus to a general desire for the improvement in the construction and discipline of prisons in Britain. Although mainly about conditions at home he also reported on what he found on his Continental travels. In most places conditions were no better, in some respects worse; for example, torture was not uncommon. Only in Holland did he find a model he could recommend for adoption at home.

In autumn of that year he was summoned before a select committee of the House of Commons appointed to enquire into the working of the hulk system, whereby dismantled ships were used as prisons. He maintained that such vessels were less suitable for the confinement of prisoners than buildings, and it was agreed that the system should be changed. In 1779 an Act was passed empowering the erection of two penitentiary houses under the superintendence of three supervisors, but nothing further was done. This was partly because Howard resigned from the special committee owing to a disagreement as to where they were to be sited; his rigid principles did not allow compromise even to a small degree. Over the next few years Howard visited prisons in Prussia, Saxony, Bohemia, Austria, Italy, Switzerland, France, Denmark, Sweden, Russia, Spain and Portugal, as well as in Britain.

After all this activity Howard, approaching sixty, settled again at Cardington, apparently with no plans for further travels. He had seen little of his son John for some years. As a child John had been expected to obey instantly his father's every wish. He grew up a fine, tall, pleasing lad, ready for university. His father sent him first to Edinburgh but found the young man quickly fell into bad company. Then he tried Cambridge, which was not far from Cardington. John was admitted as a fellow-commoner at St John's College, where a friend of his father's agreed to watch over his conduct. Satisfied that his son was in good hands the father now prepared for another philanthropic tour. This time his objective was to visit the seaports, where attempts were made to try to prevent the spread of the plague by confining new arrivals in secure hospitals, called lazarettos, until it was certain they were free of the disease.

Howard set out on his expedition in November, and though refused permission to inspect the lazaretto at Marseilles he still managed to do so. In order to obtain access to the one at Toulon he adopted the disguise of a fashionable Parisian. He went on to visit Nice, Genoa, Leghorn, Pisa, Florence, Rome and Naples. From Naples he proceeded to Malta, Zante, Smyrna and Constantinople. Resolving to subject himself to the discipline of quarantine he purposely chose a vessel bound for Venice with a foul bill of health. After leaving the Morea, they had a skirmish with a Tunisian privateer. On reaching Venice Howard was confined in lazarettos for six weeks. He was shocked by the conditions in which those under quarantine were held, but he took the opportunity to learn from the physicians in charge what they knew about the spread of the disease and subsequently published a report on the defects of the lazaretto system.

On his return to England he found that some of his supporters had established a fund to erect a statue in his honour. Howard firmly declined the honour and insisted that any funds collected be used for the benefit of prisoners. Uncomfortable with his celebrity status, he refused portrait sittings. 'As a private man,' he explained, 'with some peculiarities, I wish to remain in obscurity and silence.' In Cardington, however, he found that while he was abroad his son John had led a profligate life and turned his father's house into a centre of debauchery: one of the many exploits that young Howard and his friends indulged in was to disturb a congregation of dissenters, and attempt to break up their religious meeting. Worse, the young man had developed a violent temper, and was showing signs of paranoia. Before long he became mentally deranged and was confined in a private asylum, where he died hopelessly insane at the age of 34. It is now thought he suffered from cerebral syphilis, but at the time it was held by some that the harsh treatment he received from his father as a boy was responsible. Friends of the family thought John had experienced too much discipline and too little parental affection. Howard's idea of family discipline was said to be severe in the extreme. To the boy he represented authority untempered by a show of affection and humour, a father whose love, if it existed, was never apparent. He had never been a man of warmth, rather a man of determination, obstinate in doing what he thought right, whatever the opposition. He was not a friendly man, given to discussion and personal persuasion, but one who, though not impressive physically, liked to dominate in debate. The desire for dominance in personal relationships developed increasingly within him, making warm cooperation with men who sympathised with his schemes impossible.

In 1789 Howard set out on his last journey, not expecting ever to see his homeland again. 'I do not have long to live,' he told his friends. He made his will leaving everything to good causes, after providing for his unfortunate son. He said goodbye to his servants and the villagers of Cardington. This time he visited Holland, Germany, Prussia, Livonia and finally Russia. The defective state of the Russian military hospitals attracted his attention, and hearing in Moscow of the sickly state of the Russian army on the confines of Turkey, he proceeded to the new Black Sea port of Cherson being created in the Crimea. He died there on 20 January 1790 from typhus caught while in attendance on a young lady with the disease. A brick pyramid was built over his grave and a handsome cenotaph of white freestone with Russian inscription was erected in his memory at Cherson. In England memorials were erected in London and Bedford.

Howard was a man of deeply religious feeling, with an observant mind and methodical habits. He was both a teetotaller and a vegetarian, simple in his tastes, plain and neat in his dress. From the day he entered into the duties of the High Sheriff of Bedfordshire he devoted himself almost entirely to his philanthropic labours. Though not gifted with any brilliant talents, he possessed a powerful will, great pertinacity of purpose, and remarkable powers of endurance. He worked unaided by the state or by charitable institutions, spending more than £30,000 of his own money on philanthropic work. Constituting himself inspector of prisons at home and abroad, he travelled upwards of fifty thousand miles, notebook in hand, visiting prisons, hospitals, lazarettos, schools and workhouses. According to Aikin (1792):

> In stature John Howard was below average in height, thin and spare in build, rather mean and forbidding in appearance, of somewhat sallow complexion, the nose prominent, the glance penetrating. There was also a vivacity in his manner, an alertness in his gait, an animation in his gesture, which fully confirmed the activity of his mental powers. But with these were united a softness – verging on an effeminacy of voice – a gentleness of demeanour, an indescribable sweetness and benevolence in his smile, which tempered the harsher gestures, and sobered the

livelier casts of expression in his intelligent face and characteristic air. Such was the energy of his nature that whatever he took in hand he accomplished in as complete and perfect a manner as it was possible for human exertion to attain; having once bent all the faculties of his mind, and every energy of his being, to one defined point, nothing could divert him from following it with the same constancy and intensity of purpose as though it had been the sole end of his existence.

Howard described his good works as his 'hobby' or his 'whim'. He used to say, 'I am the plodder who goes about collecting materials for men of genius to make use of.' He was rather a man of detail, of laborious accuracy and minute examination. In manner and in dress, he was said to be 'somewhat precise'. Contemporaries described him as deporting himself in a sober, rigid, old-fashioned way. According to one of them, Howard was rather pragmatical in his speech, very polite, but expressing himself in a manner which seemed to belong to two hundred years before. Once he was determined on something, he was unyielding to any persuasion or dissuasion, and pressed on to the accomplishment of his purpose regardless of obstacles. Aikin, who was a medical man, portrays Howard as rather a priggish man of 'scruples and singularities' who, while observing the obligatory forms of social life, eschewed its more relaxed and spontaneous aspects. 'His sobriety of manners and peculiarities of living did not fit him for much promiscuous society' (Aikin 1792). Punctual to the minute in every engagement he made, he usually sat down when in conversation, with his watch in his hand, which he rested upon his knee, and though in the midst of an interesting anecdote or argument, so soon as the moment he had fixed on for his departure arrived, he arose, took up his hat, and left the house. He calculated also how long it would take to walk or ride to the place of his next engagement with such nicety that he was seldom a second beyond his appointment.

Howard was no sentimentalist, and while he insisted that justice should be blended with humanity, he was not against just punishment, aimed at the reformation of the prisoners. For him philanthropy was a compelling religious duty, and his writings are full of this. In religion he was a Calvinist, but he was not narrow-minded. Both his wives were Anglicans, while many of his friends were Quakers. In the prisons he visited he was concerned that consumption of alcohol should be forbidden, likewise gambling, and that a chaplain should visit regularly. He was shocked when prisoners of both sexes were confined together. Although he would sometimes try to help individuals he encountered, he was mainly concerned with collecting information about the prisons he visited, interrogating the authorities, counting the steps, measuring the rooms, taking copies of the regulations, and testing the supplies. Insensitivity to the feelings of others emerges in Howard's account of an incident that occurred during a visit to a Swedish prison. After watching the severe punishment of a male and female prisoner, Howard observed that both seemed only just alive, the man especially, and 'they had barely sufficient strength left to evince signs of gratitude on my giving them a small donation'. His benevolence was always entirely impersonal.

Recently the psychiatrist Philip Lucas (2001) re-examined the available materials and came to the conclusion that Howard suffered from Asperger's syndrome. Aikin (1792) states that '[Howard's] stern views of duty frequently prevented him from being a very sociable companion'; this indicates problems of social interaction. Howard's role as a self-appointed prison visitor would fulfil the requirement of an all-absorbing narrow interest pattern. As for routines and rituals, we can cite Aikin's statement that 'He was a lover of regularity in all his affairs and was particularly noted for strict punctuality and for the exact and methodical disposition of time.' For peculiarities of speech and language we are told that his voice verged on the effeminate, and for problems of non-verbal communication, we have the statement that his gaze was penetrating. According to Lucas, Howard's impairments of social communication are evident only in private letters, since he delegated the writing of his reports and books to trusted aides. It seems possible that his father might also have had the disorder, but we know too little about him.

Acknowledgment

The principal sources of information in this chapter are Aikin (1792), Brown (1823), Field (1850), Lucas (2001), Howard (1958) and Southward (1958).

CHAPTER SIX

Henry Cavendish (1731–1810)

He seemed to consider himself as a solitary being in the world, and to feel himself unfit for society. (Henry, Lord Brougham 1872)

Henry Cavendish was arguably the greatest British physicist in the century after Newton.

Sacks (2001b) writes that 'in the case of Cavendish the evidence [of autism]…is almost overwhelming'. Baron-Cohen (cited in James 2003b) says:

> there are clues that Cavendish may have had some degree of Asperger's syndrome. He shows abnormalities in social relationships, communication, and some routine-bound repetitive behavior. We must assume that his scientific pursuits were strongly obsessional in nature. However, missing from the historical record are any details of his childhood.

This is often a problem, even with people of not so long ago; biographers do not always regard this kind of information as significant.

Henry Cavendish was born into the nobility. His father, Lord Charles Cavendish, was the third son of the second Duke of Devonshire; his mother, Lady Anne Grey, was the fourth daughter of Henry, Duke of Kent. She was living in Nice, owing to frail health, when Henry was born on 10 October 1731; a second child Frederick

was born in England two years later, but their mother died shortly afterwards. Little is known of the early years of the two boys, except that they attended the Hackney Academy, a London school well thought of in its day for the education of children of the upper classes in sound classical learning. Each of the brothers went up to Cambridge, matriculated as a nobleman, resided for four years but left without taking a degree. The college to which they belonged was St Peter's, commonly known as Peterhouse. Shortly after the younger brother left Cambridge, they made the customary tour on the Continent together, but afterwards they saw little of each other.

After returning to England Henry Cavendish went to live with his father in Great Marlborough Street, in the Soho district of London. Lord Charles was a gifted experimental physicist, who made some valuable investigations into heat, electricity and terrestrial magnetism. Henry began his research career by assisting his father, and apparently continued to do so until Lord Charles died. It was during this period of almost thirty years that his son carried out the fundamental electrical research for which he is renowned. Long after his death, when Clerk Maxwell was editing his papers for publication, he found twenty packages of fascinating manuscripts on mathematical and experimental electricity, in which Henry Cavendish had quietly anticipated many of the fundamental results discovered in the nineteenth century.

Although the Cavendishes were wealthy, Lord Charles was not rich and the financial allowance he made to his elder son was quite niggardly. In 1783, when his father died, or even before, Henry Cavendish somehow became extremely wealthy, apparently through a succession of legacies from relatives, but by this time he had become accustomed to living parsimoniously. He had built himself a house on Bedford Square, just round the corner from the British Museum, where he displayed his vast collection of minerals and a large library of scientific works, open to any serious scholars. At one time this was in a somewhat neglected state, so having been told of a needy German scholar who was capable of classifying the books in a satisfactory manner, Cavendish arranged for him to act as librarian; in return Cavendish gave him the princely sum of £10,000 with which to purchase an annuity.

Cavendish's principal laboratory was a large villa in the rural London suburb of Clapham. Most of its rooms were equipped with scientific apparatus. It was at Clapham that he made his discovery of the chemical composition of water, and measured by means of a torsion balance the density of the earth. The grounds contained an eighty-foot telescope, with which he made astronomical observations. He was very much a man of habit, invariably dining off leg of mutton, and taking exactly the same solitary walk every day, wearing a three-cornered hat. His pathologically shy and nervous disposition, which anyone who had any contact with him was apt to remark, has been attributed to his comparative poverty in the first forty years of his life, but can be explained much better by the Asperger hypothesis.

Cavendish was tall and thin, the expression on his face intelligent and mild. His voice was hesitant and somewhat shrill, indicating problems of speech and language. He walked with a slight stoop, like other members of the Cavendish family. He would often be accompanied by the physician and scientist Charles Blagden, later secretary of the Royal Society, who for seven years acted as his personal assistant. In his diary Blagden frequently describes Cavendish as 'sulky'. When eventually Cavendish parted with Blagden's services he provided him with an annuity of £500 and left him a legacy of £15,000 in his will.

Cavendish's interests extended over a wide field of natural philosophy, and every subject of investigation was subjected to a rigorous quantitative examination. The results he obtained with simple methods and apparatus are amazing. Not only was he a highly skilled experimentalist but also a capable mathematician. In common with others in England at this period, he employed the methods of Newton; like Newton he had a deep dislike of controversy. As a result he published remarkably little, for example only two research papers on electricity, although he wrote up his work meticulously.

Although Cavendish mainly lived as a recluse owing to a morbid dislike of society, he nevertheless participated in the intellectual life of London. He was a member of the Royal Society of Arts, a trustee of the British Museum, a fellow of the Society of Antiquaries, a manager of the Royal Institution, and a foreign associate of the Paris Academy. Like his father before him he was prominent in the Royal Society, to which he was elected in 1760, served on the Council and some of its committees, and regularly attended the Dining Club, to which he often took guests. The only known portrait of him, now in the British Museum, was drawn surreptitiously at one of the club dinners. It was useless to try to engage him in conversation on any non-scientific topic, but when he chose to speak what he said was 'luminous and profound'. According to a contemporary, his speech was always 'exceeding to the purpose, and either brought some excellent information, or drew some important conclusions'. Apart from science his only interest was music.

The jurist Henry, later Lord, Brougham (1872) recalled seeing him at a Royal Society conversazione and hearing 'the shrill cry he uttered as he shuffled quickly from room to room, seeming to be annoyed if looked at, but sometimes approaching to hear what was passing among others'. His slouching walk was quick and uneasy, suggestive of motor clumsiness. Brougham continued: 'He probably uttered fewer words in the course of his life than any man who lived to fourscore years, not at all excepting the monks of La Trappe.' Other contemporaries recalled: 'He was the coldest and most indifferent of mortals,' 'He was shy and bashful to a degree bordering on disease,'

'He could not bear to have any person introduced to him, or to be pointed out in any way as a remarkable man.'

For most of Cavendish's adult life the head of the family was the indolent fifth Duke of Devonshire. His first wife Georgiana, who was Cavendish's cousin-in-law, and queen of London society, was keenly interested in music, literature, history and science, and Cavendish may have acted as her scientific tutor. But generally his attitude to the female sex was dismissive. The Royal Society Club met in a certain tavern; a member recalled:

> One evening we observed a very pretty girl looking out from an upper window on the opposite side of the street, watching the philosophers at dinner. She attracted notice, and one by one we got up and mustered round the window to admire the fair one. Cavendish, who thought we were looking at the moon, bustled up to us in his odd way, and when he saw the real object of our study, turned away with intense disgust, and grunted out 'Pshaw!'
> (Jungnickel and McCormmack 1999)

Cavendish died on 24 February 1810, at the age of seventy-eight, and was buried in the Cavendish mausoleum of All Saints Church, Derby, where two centuries earlier his famous ancestor, the proud and acquisitive Elizabeth Countess of Shrewsbury (Bess of Hardwick), had been laid to rest. Owing to his frugal lifestyle her descendant had accumulated a fortune of over a million pounds, a massive sum in those days. When he died none of this wealth went directly to support scientific research; he believed it should return to the family from which it came. However, many years later his university benefited from the generosity of the Cavendish family through the endowment by the eighth Duke of Devonshire of the Cavendish professorship of experimental physics and the Cavendish laboratory.

In his memoir *Uncle Tungsten* (2001a) the neurologist Oliver Sacks digresses at one point to describe the excellent early biography (1851) of Cavendish by George Wilson as 'the fullest account we are ever likely to have of the life and mind of a unique autistic genius'. A more recent biography by Christa Jungnickel and Russell McCormmack (1999) adds something to what Wilson tells us about Cavendish's life and work. They comment that his life was his science and that 'he had two rather forbidding traits...a pathological fear of strangers that could render him speechless, and a clockwork regularity in all his transactions with life'. They observe that he had a number of autistic-like traits: single-mindedness, apparent inability to feel certain emotions, secludedness, rigidities of behaviour, odd gait, harsh voice, strange vocalisations, panic attacks and self-acknowledged social unfitness.

Sacks (2001b) summarises the characteristics of his peculiar personality as follows:

> Even in his lifetime, his peculiarities were the stuff of legend. He did all his work alone, in complete solitude, in the extraordinary laboratory he built in his house. He rarely spoke to anyone, and insisted that his servants communicate with him in writing. He was indifferent to fame and fortune (though he was the grandson of a duke, and for much of his life one of the richest men in England) and seems to have had little comprehension of the value of money. He published only a fraction of his results. Completely uninterested in the competition, the rivalries which are so common in science, he showed only indifference when Antoine-Laurent Lavoisier and others claimed priority for discoveries that he himself had made years before.

Acknowledgment

The biographical information in this chapter is based on James (2003a). The other principal sources of information in this chapter are Berry (1960), Jungnickel and McCormmack (1999) and Wilson (1851).

CHAPTER SEVEN

Thomas Jefferson (1743–1826)

A nation's chief executive greeting dignitaries while dressed in odd frayed clothing, worn-out bedroom slippers, his hair uncombed, at times with a pet mocking-bird perched on his shoulder, was not what I would regard as normal. (Norm Ledgin)

We turn now to America, where one of the Founding Fathers of the United States shows clear signs of having had the syndrome. Thomas Jefferson was perhaps the most complex person ever to hold the office of president. So much has been written about him, with new books appearing frequently, that the reader is sure to be familiar with the main features of his life. Yet his character has puzzled many of his biographers, and the Asperger hypothesis, recently proposed by Norm Ledgin (2000), might serve to explain at least some of his idiosyncracies. The following profile is largely based on what Ledgin has written, which in turn is based on the Jefferson biography *American Sphinx* by J.J. Ellis (1997), although Ellis would not have known of Ledgin's suggestion. The personal information that has been discovered about Jefferson shows clearly that his behaviour matched the standard criteria for an assessment of Asperger's syndrome. Temple Grandin has added a note to Ledgin's book agreeing with his suggestion.

Peter Jefferson, the father of the future president, was of Welsh ancestry. Although of education 'quite neglected', he was a man of rugged vitality. He conducted the first survey of the State of Virginia, and profiting by the knowledge this gave him became a wealthy landowner. After his death in 1757 his widow and eight children inherited large estates and slaves to work on them. Thomas Jefferson was the elder of his two sons. His mother Jane (née Randolph) came from one of the grander families of the Old Dominion. When Thomas started writing his autobiography towards the end of his life, an exercise that people with Asperger's tend to find particularly difficult, he had much to say about his father, but very little about his mother. Elisabeth, one of their other children, was said to be feeble-minded; she drowned in a boating accident before she reached the age of thirty. Furthermore, Jefferson's younger brother was quite slow and persistently childlike. Some of the Randolphs were unstable and idiosyncratic; if Thomas had Asperger's it seems most likely to have come from that side of the family.

The future president was born on 13 April 1743. His early schooling included Latin, Greek, French and mathematics. We know that he was bullied, like most boys with Asperger's, and that the school friends he chose were not of his own age. He went on to the College of

William and Mary at Williamsburg, where he continued his mathematical studies and became interested in science; later he was to say that if
he had been unable to make a career in politics, he would have become
a scientist. After graduation he qualified as a lawyer and in 1767 began
to practise as an attorney in Williamsburg. Already he was keeping a
record of the minutiae of his expenditures, a habit he continued for the
rest of his life. Another lifetime preoccupation was the construction of
a mansion on top of a hill he called Monticello, for which the ground
was levelled in 1768. Two years later there was a fire at Shadwell, his
birthplace in the foothills of the Blue Ridge Mountains, following
which he left the family home and began to live in the part of his new
house that was ready for occupation. In the fire almost all the papers
that would have thrown light on his early life were destroyed.

Jefferson was a tall man, the face lean, the eyes hazel, the mouth
thin, the chin sharp, the coppery hair full and thick. In 1772 he
married Martha Wayles Skelton, the widowed daughter of a law colleague, who brought him an ample dowry. She was said to be full of
good humour, and to have shared his love of music. A son by her
previous marriage died before the wedding, but within ten months
they had a daughter and eventually six children. When his wife died in
childbirth in 1782 he went into paroxysms of grief, burnt all her
letters to him, and continued to worship her memory for the rest of his
life. Only two of their children reached adulthood; a younger
daughter Maria died at the age of twenty-five so that Martha, the
first-born, was Jefferson's only surviving child. Jefferson was a father
who loved his daughters but could not bring himself to hug them.

There was a mulatto slave family named Hemings working in his
household. One of them, Elisabeth, had a daughter, Sally, by the father
of Jefferson's late wife, and so Sally was Martha's half-sister. Jefferson's
cohabitation with Sally lasted almost thirty-eight years. She had
several children and the possibility that one or more of them was his
has been the subject of much speculation. Jefferson depended on slaves
for his economic existence; there were usually around one hundred on
his various properties. He treated them relatively well, and promised

that they would not be sold without their consent and that they would be given their freedom when he died.

Jefferson had entered politics in his early thirties. While his personal views were progressive, even radical, it was impossible to build a political career in reactionary Virginia on that basis. As a delegate from the Old Dominion Jefferson played a decisive role in the Continental Congress that drafted the Declaration of Independence. He served as governor of his home state from 1779 for a two-year term, at the end of which he wrote a book, *Notes on the State of Virginia*, the first comprehensive study of any part of the United States. After the death of his wife he went to Paris to succeed Benjamin Franklin as a representative of his country. He took the opportunity to tour Europe and observe new advances in technology that could be introduced in America. While he was in Paris, he had an extended liaison with a married woman.

Five years later he returned home at the age of fifty-one, expecting to be left to enjoy a quiet retirement on his estate at Monticello. Instead he was appointed Secretary of State in the Washington administration and then, in a crucial election, became the third president of the United States in 1800. In the four years he held office his most notable achievement was the Louisiana purchase, the huge land acquisition from France that almost doubled the size of the nation. These were eventful years in early American history, but even a brief account would hardly be germane to my main theme.

In 1809 Jefferson withdrew from public life and at last settled down in Monticello, the house that had been under construction, on and off, for most of his life. By this time his main preoccupation had become the foundation at Charlottesville of the University of Virginia. He intended this to be a rival to the northern universities of Harvard and Yale, in which Southern values would be upheld. He took a very detailed interest in almost every aspect of the new institution, for example personally cataloguing all 6860 books in the library. He was concerned that the students should be quartered with 'quasi-parents'. His activities when creating the University of Virginia had an obsessive character.

Unfortunately, although he always kept detailed records of all his personal expenditure, Jefferson was quite incapable of understanding that for many years his income had fallen far short of his expenditure. Moreover he unwisely guaranteed a large loan to a friend, who defaulted. As a result Jefferson became insolvent and, when he died on 4 July 1826, the Monticello house and estate, together with many of his slaves, had to be sold as part of the settlement of his enormous debts.

Jefferson was a very kind and generous man, gracious, polite and diplomatic. He had a marvellously keen mind, but was considered unduly sensitive to criticism. He took greatest pride in three accomplishments that had nothing to do with his presidency – authorship of both the Declaration of Independence and the Statute of Virginia for Religious Freedom, and the foundation of the University of Virginia. He ordered only these three accomplishments to be inscribed on his tombstone, which bears no mention of his other political services to the Union and his home state. He was certainly the most prolific of chief executives as a writer and political philosopher, and his interests the most wide-ranging; they included the natural sciences, agriculture, botany, zoology, cartography, diplomacy, ethnology, meteorology, archaeology, surveying, technology, architecture, languages and the law. However, the peculiar patterns of behaviour that we are studying must have placed many difficulties in his path. Guided by Ledgin (2000), let us consider some of these.

Jefferson had peculiarities of speech and language; in Congress he never made a speech, and in fact seldom spoke more than a few words. His speaking skills were so poor that even in the second row, listeners had to wait for the next day's newspaper to learn what he had said. When he wanted to raise his voice in volume it tended to sink lower in pitch and made him inarticulate. Once, when he approached a young woman to announce his feelings towards her, he delivered much of what he planned to say in a disordered manner, with long frequent pauses. She was unimpressed and shortly afterwards became engaged to someone else.

Jefferson also had sensory problems common to people with Asperger's – a hypersensitivity to the sound of voices mixing in conversation and voices raised in argument, and a hyposensitivity to loud sounds in his nailery at Monticello. He explained that his hearing was distinct in particular conversation but confused when several people voiced across each other, which 'unfits me for the society of the table'. He was said to be a good story-teller but not much of a conversationalist. He was a man who fled from the company of others to read or write, sometimes for fifteen hours a day. Although he had many friends, there was a lack of reciprocity in the relationships; he liked people to come to him rather than he to them. In his official work he lacked patience with social hierarchies. He tried to avoid the rough and tumble of life as far as possible.

Jefferson was conspicuously awkward in gestures while standing to listen or speak, and awkward while seated at meetings. In his youth he was said to have been more awkward than graceful in his movements, suggestive of motor clumsiness, and one of his contemporaries observed that he barely moved his arms while walking. Jefferson required soft clothing on certain parts of his body – waist, hips, legs and feet – but tight clothing across his chest for calming pressure there. Rather like John Howard he believed he could ward off infection by plunging his feet into cold water every morning. He liked to sing or hum music to himself while he was thinking. 'He is a man of science,' said one of his contemporaries, 'but he knows little of the nature of man – very little indeed.'

In his biography, Ellis wrote that Jefferson was capable of reasoning along two tracks. Interior defences protected him from realities he did not want to face, such as his dependency on slaves and his declining financial condition. He thought of the world in terms of black and white, ignoring the middle ground for resolving conflicts. His contemporaries tended to disregard his peculiarities because he was a man with so many redeeming qualities. While devoted to the ideal of improving mankind he showed comparatively little interest in particular people. It is no insult to his memory to suggest that the Asperger hypothesis accounts better than anything else for much that is otherwise puzzling in his character.

Acknowledgment

The principal sources of information in this chapter are Ellis (1997) and Ledgin (2000).

CHAPTER EIGHT

Vincent van Gogh (*1853–1890*)

As a child not only were his brother and sisters strangers to him, he was a stranger to himself. (Elizabeth van Gogh)

After Michelangelo, several other artists have been suggested as Asperger possibles, for example Vassily Kandinski, Maurice Utrillo and L.S. Lowry. A profile of Andy Warhol, a particularly strong possibility, will be given later (Chapter 19). Although it may be impossible to reach any firm conclusion, it is particularly difficult to resist discussing the case of Vincent van Gogh. Like those of his contemporary Paul Cézanne, his paintings, virtually unsaleable in his lifetime, now fetch astronomical prices. His tragic decline into madness has never been fully explained, although his unhappy life has been the subject of many biographies. He was a man whose psychological conflicts entered into all aspects of his development and whose positive use of them was essential to his triumph as an artist. His influence on modern painting has been enormous.

The Reverend Theodorus van Gogh and Anna Cornelia Carbentus married in 1851. Their first child died at birth. Their second, the future painter, was born on 30 March 1853, and christened Vincent Willem. Their other children were Anna in 1855, Theodore in 1857, Elizabeth in 1859, Wilhelmina in 1862, and finally Cornelius in 1867. Of the siblings, it was Theo who played a major role in Vincent's life, Wilhelmina a very minor one, the others hardly any. Two

years before his marriage, Pastor van Gogh had been called to the modest living of Zundert, a large village in North Brabant, surrounded by depressing countryside. The parents were accustomed to a life of austerity and self-denial, but had high hopes for their sons. Their father, an undistinguished pastor of the Dutch Reformed Church, ministered to the needs of a small flock; most of the villagers were Catholics. The dominant parent was his wife, an intelligent, determined woman who was clever at drawing and watercolour painting, and knowledgeable about botany. She was said to be rather cold and have a 'dark nature'. She had been brought up in The Hague, where her father was a bookbinder. Vincent's paternal grandfather was a prominent citizen of Breda: he was a senior minister in the Church, but of his six sons only Theodorus, the father of Vincent, followed his example; three of the others became art dealers, another became an admiral, the last a civil servant. He also had two daughters, both of whom married senior army officers.

We do not know much about Vincent's childhood. One of the former servants in the household said he never behaved like a child; he looked back on his childhood as gloomy, cold and sterile. He took after his mother in appearance, perhaps also in personality. He was intensely serious, earnest and unsmiling, silent and morose, ugly and uncouth. He had no social life, but would wander off on his own. His sister Wilhelmina gave a description of his youthful appearance as follows:

> Broad rather than tall, his back slightly bent owing to a bad habit of letting his head hang forward, his reddish hair cut short beneath a straw hat which overshadowed his unusual face: not at all the face of a boy. His brow was already slightly wrinkled, his eyebrows drawn together in deep thought across the wide forehead, his eyes small and deep-set, sometimes blue, at other times green, according to his changing expressions. Despite this unattractive, awkward appearance, there was yet something remarkable in his unmistakeable expression of inward profundity. (Erpel 1965)

After a period at the village school, van Gogh was sent to a small boarding school at Zevenberg, nineteen miles from Zundert, where the teacher offered French, English, German, mathematics and social sciences. Being attached to his family, he was upset to be parted from them. After two years he was transferred to a similar establishment at Tilburn, where he stayed for eighteen months. His formal education ceased abruptly in March 1868, when he was fifteen, and he was at home for the next fifteen months. After a family conference he was sent off to The Hague at the end of July 1869 to learn about art dealing at the firm of Goupil et Fils, in which one of his uncles was a partner. We know that his mother arranged for him to lodge with a family named Roos, comfortably middle class, kindly but somewhat dull. We have little information about what van Gogh was doing, except that Theodore (Theo), four years his junior, came to stay and the two brothers made a vow of friendship. The articulate and poignant correspondence between them is an abundant source of information about van Gogh's later life and his aesthetic aims. Next van Gogh was transferred to Goupil's London division, with an excellent testimonial; there is no doubt that he was successful as a trainee art dealer. The first few months of the year he spent in London seem to have been the happiest of his life. When the firm gave him a rise in salary he was able to help his parents by sending some money home. He lodged at Kennington and walked to and from the office each day. His landlady, the widow of a clergyman, had a daughter Ursula who served at table. Van Gogh fell in love with her and proposed marriage. He was shocked to be told that she was secretly engaged to another man, who had boarded at the house before van Gogh arrived. He became distraught, lost interest in his work, and took up Bible reading. When he started being impolite to customers he was transferred to the Paris branch of Goupil's, where his uncle could keep an eye on him. But his behaviour was so unacceptable that he was asked to leave the firm in April 1876.

Meanwhile van Gogh's father had been transferred to Etten, still in Brabant, and so the family were now living there. Vincent told his parents he had turned his back on commerce; what he wanted to do now was teach and become a lay preacher. He soon found a post at a small private school run by a pedantic Methodist minister named Stokes in the English coastal town of Ramsgate, Kent. This gave him a chance to perfect his English. Always a great walker, one weekend he set out to walk to London, a considerable distance. He liked to walk at night, especially when feeling depressed. When Stokes moved his school to Isleworth, further up the Thames, van Gogh was given opportunities to preach at nearby chapels. His sincerity was apparent but his speech was halting, his voice deep and melancholy, his use of language awkward and his delivery poor. When Stokes asked him to go round collecting school fees from parents who could ill afford them, he resigned from the school and returned to Holland.

Again there was a family conference, which led to him being found a position as clerk in a bookshop in Dordrecht. Although he knew nothing of the book trade, he was courteous towards customers. When not otherwise occupied he spent his time translating the New Testament of the Bible from a Dutch text into English, French and German. Increasingly he was feeling a strong religious vocation. To become a minister, like his father, he needed to study theology at university, which required some knowledge of Latin and Greek. One of the uncles undertook to help him, by arranging for private tuition in Amsterdam. After a good start at the ancient languages van Gogh became obsessed with the idea that his vocation was to preach the

Gospel to the poor. So there was another change of plan and he began studying at a school for missionaries in Brussels, where a knowledge of the classics was not required. His tutor reported repeated episodes of self-flagellation and, on his face, an expression of indescribable sadness and despair.

When his probationary period at the school was over, the committee on evangelisation told him he was unsuitable for missionary work. It was said he was short on humility and that he was also not much good at public speaking, an ability that the school regarded as essential to a missionary. Van Gogh was devastated at this setback to his plans. Although unqualified, he could still act as a lay evangelist. There was a coalfield in the southwest of Belgium near Mons, the Borinage, somewhat like the grim world written about by Emile Zola in *Germinal*. He spent twenty-two months in this black country, giving Bible readings and visiting the sick. He dressed like a tramp, and lived on a starvation diet; there was a strong masochistic streak in his personality. Impressed by his zeal the missionary school committee relented and he was given a temporary post in nearby Wasmes. Although at no time in his life did he show that he wanted to involve himself in the socialist movements of the day, the evangelisation committee began to feel he was identifying himself too greatly with the down-trodden colliers and their families. While praising his devotion and self-sacrifice in tending to the sick and wounded, they decided he was such an indifferent preacher as to render the evangelist's principal function wholly impossible.

Meanwhile van Gogh was assiduously making charcoal drawings of the colliers, peasants and other labourers. It was at this point that he seems to have started, at the age of twenty-nine, to consider the possibility of a vocation in art, and to make this 'the means by which he could bring consolation to humanity'. 'I cannot tell you how happy I am to have taken up drawing again,' he wrote to Theo. 'I have recovered my mental balance, and day by day my energy increases' (van Gogh 1988). Van Gogh had seen many first-class paintings and other works of art in his time at Goupil's. However, although he had learned something from books, he was lacking in the practical education an artist needs. To find better working conditions, he moved to Brussels for six months, where his brother Theo had entered the Brussels branch of Goupil's after leaving college. Van Gogh found an experienced painter who was willing to give him some lessons in perspective. He also applied for a place at the Académie des Beaux Arts, which would have enabled him to attend life classes free of charge; whether he ever did so is uncertain.

In April 1881 van Gogh decided to return to Etten and spend Easter with the family, where his mother still dominated the household. Although his reappearances were greeted with some dismay he enjoyed being at home again. Of his sisters only Wilhelmina, the youngest, was prepared to pose for him. By now he was turning out drawings at a great rate, but had not yet started painting. A recently widowed cousin named Kee from Amsterdam came to stay, with her four-year-old son. Van Gogh fell in love with her and proposed marriage, but was summarily rejected. Again he felt devastated. She refused to see him when he pursued her to Amsterdam, but he never forgot her.

By August 1882 van Gogh felt his drawing skills had progressed far enough for him to begin painting in oils. Antoine Mauve, a cousin by marriage who was an established painter in The Hague, agreed to initiate him in the mysteries of the palette. Mauve was temperamental but gave van Gogh some encouragement. When van Gogh ran out of money he returned to Etten but then quarrelled with his father, and went back to The Hague, increasingly determined to prove himself as a painter. He tried watercolour, but it was drawing that inspired him at this stage. To earn a living he tried to produce drawings of the type that would sell to the illustrated papers. As usual his brother Theo was helpful; he tactfully sent van Gogh money regularly through their father, which made it more acceptable.

In his letters to Theo, van Gogh told of his encounter with a warm-hearted prostitute, apparently his first such experience. The next woman in his life was Clasina Maria Hoornik, three years his senior, who he met casually in 1882. She was an alcoholic who supplemented her wages as a cleaner by prostitution, as her mother had done. She had a five-year-old daughter, and was pregnant. He shared his room with Sien, as he called her, and her young daughter. They were an additional expense but at least he had willing models. His first major pictures dating from this period in the capital are of Sien. Somehow this inadequate woman gave him confidence in himself. He was devoted to her, and began to talk of marriage. Then van Gogh had a spell in hospital being treated for gonorrhoea while Sien gave birth to a boy. After recovering from post-natal depression, she began to quarrel with him.

In mid-September 1883, van Gogh and Sien had an emotional parting when van Gogh went off to Drenthe, a remote moorland region in the north of Holland. The featureless landscape, broken only by canals, was starting to attract artists. He enjoyed the four rainy months he spent there before returning for Christmas to the parental home, now near a place called Nuenen. There was the usual row with his father. He made an agreement with his brother that, in return for his entire artistic production, Theo would pay him a monthly allowance of 150 francs. He stayed on at Nuenen for two years, turning out work at a tremendous rate. When his mother moved to Breda in 1886, after her husband died, she took with her 60 of his paintings on stretchers, 150 loose canvases, 90 pen drawings and a large number of crayon drawings. Unfortunately she found traces of woodworm in the packing cases in which they were stored and threw many of them out. Even so, those that survived amounted to 225 drawings, 25 watercolours and 185 oils, mostly of a dark and sombre character. One was his first masterpiece, *The Potato Eaters.*

In November 1885 van Gogh moved to Antwerp and enrolled in the Academy of Fine Arts. Japanese woodblock prints had just begun to arrive in the West. Most of the first wave of modern painters were influenced by these prints, but in van Gogh's case the influence was particularly strong. He was also able to study the masterpieces of Rubens and learn how to make better use of colour. However, van Gogh's aim was to join his brother Theo, who was working in Paris, so after three months he departed from his homeland and moved to France, where he would spend the rest of his life. In Paris van Gogh not only stayed with his brother but also started to use his small apartment as a workshop; consequently they moved to a much larger one in Montmartre. There he met the Impressionist painters, including Edouard Degas, Paul Gauguin, Georges Seurat and Henri de Toulouse-Lautrec. However, the most important artistic contact was Camille Pissarro, who shared his admiration for Jean-Francois Millet, the 'peasant painter'. Van Gogh followed his example by painting and drawing labourers at work. In contrast to the dark, sombre works of his Dutch period, his paintings became bright and colourful. After van Gogh's death Pissarro said, 'I always knew he would either surpass us all or end up as a madman. I never thought he would do both.'

Van Gogh's history of mental instability and physical deprivation had given him a narrow, haunted look. Those who knew him at this time remembered the red hair, of course, the rough moustache, the goatee beard, and the eagle eye. They described his lively gestures and jerky step, indicating motor clumsiness. In speech he was said to be vehement but not argumentative. He would go on and on about something, then stop and glance back over his shoulder while hissing through his teeth. He had begun to drink heavily, both wine and, more ominously, absinthe. For some time he had been thinking of leaving the city and moving somewhere further south, where the living would be cheaper and far less fraught. He set off, with characteristic suddenness, in late February 1888. Intending to go to Marseilles, he got off the train at the Provençal town of Arles. There had just been a heavy fall of snow. The flat landscape reminded him of his homeland, and he settled down. He painted many scenes from the countryside, notably *Orchards in Bloom*, as well as urban scenes, especially cafes. In the one year he lived in Arles he also painted 46 portraits of 23 different people, including a number of self-portraits. It has been suggested that it was because he abandoned any thought of women, marriage and family that he was able to produce such a very large number of works of art during the last two and a half years of his life. His health, which had been deteriorating in Paris, began to improve, although he was still drinking and smoking heavily.

Van Gogh had plans to establish a colony of fellow artists in Arles, away from the cliques and cabals of the Paris art world. When he heard that Gauguin was sick and penniless he urged him to join him in Arles. Gauguin did so, and for a short while the two painters lived together. There are signs that their relationship was partly homosexual, with van Gogh the underdog. Van Gogh's manner quickly changed from fawning obsequiousness to moody irritation, punctuated by bouts of violent anger. They had a disastrous quarrel, after which Gauguin threatened to leave.

Christmas was often a time of crisis for van Gogh. He showed his first signs of madness, made worse when Theo announced that he was engaged to be married. We have only Gauguin's account of what happened on the evening of 23 December 1888, when van Gogh took a razor and slashed at the lobe of his left ear, severing a blood vessel. He wrapped up the ear lobe and gave it to a prostitute he knew. Gauguin carried out his threat of returning to Paris, leaving van Gogh to recover from his self-inflicted injury. The junior hospital doctor who treated him thought he was over-excited but would be himself again in a few days. Two months later van Gogh was showing signs of paranoia; the local people thought he had gone mad and the police took him to the hospital in Arles. From there he was transferred to a private mental asylum in St Remy; the diagnosis was acute mania with infrequent epileptic fits, the treatment hydropathy, which just meant lying in a bath for two hours twice a week. There were dangerous outbursts of violence, but he seemed to be recovering. He was able to continue painting, and was allowed out to do so with an escort. Some of his greatest paintings date from this period.

On the recommendation of Pissarro, who at one time had worked at Auvers-sur-Oise, northwest of Paris, van Gogh came to spend the last months of his life in this attractive little town. Pissarro knew a homeopathic doctor there called Paul Gachet, who mainly practised in Paris but was a resident of Auvers, where his house was full of paintings, framed and unframed. An amateur painter himself, Gachet was one of the few patrons of the Impressionists. In medicine he specialised in mental illness, and it seemed he might be able to help van Gogh.

So on 16 May 1889 van Gogh left the asylum and went first to Paris, where he stayed with Theo, who was now married, with a baby son named Vincent. Their apartment was full of his paintings: *The Potato Eaters* in the place of honour in the dining room, *Orchards in Bloom* in the bedroom, and *Landscape from Arles* and *Night View on the Rhône* in the drawing room. They visited old haunts and five days later van Gogh went on to Auvers, as arranged. Gachet was of Flemish origin, and van Gogh got on well with him. His diagnosis was 'turpentine poisoning and too much sun'. What disturbed van Gogh about the doctor, however, was the fact that they were so much alike, both physically and mentally. He wrote to Theo 'he is sicker than I am'. Always a prodigious worker, van Gogh produced 70 oils and 30 drawings during the seventy days he was at Auvers. During his last summer, under the influence of an overwhelming depression, he painted immense expanses of wheat under troubled skies.

Meanwhile in Paris and elsewhere van Gogh's work was beginning to attract attention. Early in July he was invited to Paris to join a gathering of old friends and have lunch with Toulouse-Lautrec at Theo's apartment. Theo was in poor health and had financial problems; the art trade was in decline and his employers objected to the way he had become so involved with the Impressionists, for whose paintings there was little market. Van Gogh returned to Auvers in a disturbed state of mind. He completed one last painting, *Crows over the Wheatfield*, showing a storm-tossed cornfield out of which an ominous flight of crows is rising. Then on the evening of 27 July 1890, he borrowed a revolver, saying he was going to scare crows, but instead shot himself in the chest, clumsily but fatally. Doctors were summoned but extraction of the bullet proved impossible. He told them not to try to save his life as 'the sadness will last for ever'. Theo hurried from Paris in time to see his brother die early in the morning of 28 July, at the age of forty-seven.

Theo never recovered from the shock of his brother's death; Gauguin and Pissarro were convinced he was deranged. He died on 25 January 1891, less than six months after his brother, at the age of thirty-three. Cornelius emigrated to South Africa, only to die there, also at the age of thirty-three, possibly by his own hand. Wilhelmina, the only sister sympathetic to van Gogh, developed an incapacitating psychosis and lived in a mental home until she died in 1941 at the age of seventy-nine. However, van Gogh's mother Anna lived to a vigorous old age and outlived all her three sons, dying in 1907 at the age of eighty-six.

The precise nature of van Gogh's final illness is uncertain. Clues can be sought in his later paintings. For example, some of his later self-portraits show a dilated right pupil, indicative of glaucoma, and this is confirmed by the coloured haloes around lights he depicted in street scenes. The stars in his *Starry Night* resemble those seen in epileptic fits. Throughout his life van Gogh suffered from 'fainting fits'. Temporal lobe epilepsy has been suggested, as has poisoning by the digitalis given as treatment for the epilepsy. He was also a regular consumer of absinthe, which can produce epileptic-type convulsions and attacks of delirium. However, these occur as the result of withdrawal from absinthe; presumably this was not available to him in the asylum and yet the more serious attacks occurred when he was away from it. Other suggested diagnoses have included cerebral tumour and magnesium deficiency. Herschman and Lieb (1998) are in no doubt that he suffered from manic-depression as an adult, and according to Marie Fernicola Pennanen (1995) the most likely explanation for the diverse symptoms of his final illness is that this was accompanied by episodes of delirium caused by substance abuse.

For several siblings to have personality disorders suggests that a genetic factor was involved, possibly stemming from their mother, the dominant parent, with her cold, dark nature. According to Temple Grandin (1988), van Gogh showed clear signs of Asperger's syndrome, especially in his earlier years; the evidence for this is given above. The fact that he became emotionally involved with several women does not rule out the possibility of some degree of autism, nor does his close relationship with his brother Theo, who also suffered from recurrent depressions and became psychotic at the end of his life. In letters to Theo, Vincent wrote:

The root of the evil lies in the constitution itself, in the fatal weakening of families from generation to generation…the root of the evil lies there and there's no cure for it, in one, and in another. [Our neurosis]…is also a fatal inheritance, since in civilisation the weakness increases from generation to generation. If we want to face the real truth about our constitution we must acknowledge that we belong to the number of those who suffer from a neurosis which already had its roots in the past. (van Gogh 1988)

Acknowledgment

The principal sources of information in this chapter are Erpel (1965), Lubin (1975), Pennanen (1995), Rewald (1962) and van Gogh (1988).

CHAPTER NINE

Eric Satie
(1866–1925)

He was certainly the oddest person I have ever known, but the most brave and consistently witty person too. (Igor Stravinsky)

Nowadays Eric Satie is chiefly remembered as the composer of music that is deliberately modest and inconsequential, but in his lifetime he was also well known for his eccentricity and foolery. In his earlier compositions he was a harmonic innovator, and much of his music contains a highly purified poetry that is more than merely facetious. Although his work was severely restricted in scope, perhaps deliberately, he had an important influence on composers as varied as Claude Debussy, François Poulenc and Maurice Ravel. Fitzgerald (2003) has concluded that Satie had Asperger's; other musicians who will be profiled later are the Hungarian Béla Bartók (Chapter 12) and the Canadian Glenn Gould (Chapter 20), who have also been suggested as Asperger possibles.

Eric (or Erik) Satie was born in the busy Normandy seaport of Honfleur at the mouth of the Seine estuary, on 17 May 1866. His father Alfred Satie made a living as a shipbroker; he was an auto-didact who spoke seven languages fluently, and composed both poetry and chamber music. His mother Jane Leslie Anton was born in London of Scottish parents. Eric was one of three children: his sister Louise-Olga-Jeanne was born in 1868 and his brother Conrad the following year. After the Franco-Prussian war the family moved from

Honfleur to Paris, but two years later Eric's mother died and her sons were sent back to live with their paternal grandparents in Honfleur. While there, Eric received his first musical training, at the age of ten, from the organist of the parish church. In 1878 their grandmother also died, through drowning in strange circumstances, and Eric rejoined his father in Paris. Although his formal education was now over, his father organised some informal education for him. He had an excellent memory, read a great deal, and was to a large extent self-educated.

In 1878 his father Alfred married Eugènie Barnetsche, a piano teacher and mediocre composer whom Eric cordially disliked. She persuaded her husband that her stepson should be trained in the highly academic Paris Conservatoire. He was admitted in 1879 but dismissed three years later for failing to reach the required standard. Reports describe him as gifted but exceptionally lazy and often absent from classes. His greatest friend of the time, the Spanish-born poet Contamine de Latour, tells us that the reason he persisted with his wearisome studies was to qualify for the one-year *volontariat* in place of the normal five years of military service required of young Frenchmen. In November 1886 Eric duly joined the infantry, but after a few months he was discharged on medical grounds.

Satie's narrow bourgeois upbringing had left him shy, discreet, reserved, elegant and well-mannered. His appearance at this period in his life was that of a scruffy kind of dandy, not yet bohemian. He had begun to write music for the piano, including three sarabandes which owe a debt to Emmanuel Chabrier, whose opera *Le Roi Malgré Lui* had just had its first performance. The following year he produced his *Gymnopedies*, and in 1890, in the wake of the Paris exposition of 1889, his orientally tinged *Gnossiennes*. A voracious reader, Satie had by then developed an absorbing interest in mystical religion, Gregorian chant, Gothic art and the lives of the saints. Accompanied by de Latour he began to frequent the night-life of Montmartre. The artistic cabaret *Chat Noir* was a revelation to Satie; under the influence of its camaraderie, escapades and endless revolutionary artistic debates, his character began to evolve. Attracted to the bohemian lifestyle he moved to Montmartre.

By this time Satie was in his twenties. In the early 1890s his interest in religions led him to join an artistic movement related to the Rosicrucians. Satie became their official composer; for example, his notable 1891 piece, *Le Fils des Etoiles*, was written for them. Through this he first met the man who for some twenty-five years was to be perhaps his greatest friend, the composer Claude Debussy. 'The moment I saw him,' wrote Satie, 'I felt drawn to him and wished I could live at his side for ever.' Debussy played the role of uncle to him while in return Satie played his most characteristic role, that of jester. He knew his musical technique had severe limitations, but pride and determination, coupled with heightened sensitivity, enabled his natural humour to develop into a protective shield.

On first acquaintance Satie was amiable, well-mannered, courteous, prepossessing and very tactful.

> He listened to you, allowed you to speak, never said anything which might upset you, and was a fluent talker on every subject. It was only when you got to know him better that he let himself go with enthusiasms, changes of mood, gloomy susceptibilities and sarcasms, and showed himself to be aggressive and uneasy in his mind. (Orledge 1995)

His character was so constituted that at one time or another he had a quarrel with each of his best friends, almost always without the slightest justification. So far as is known Satie only had one love affair, a stormy one with Maurice Utrillo's mother, the painter and one-time circus performer Suzanne Valadon.

'Satie led a sad life, rather lonely,' said Darius Milhaud's wife Madeleine, who knew him well. 'He was a most lovable person, unpredictable, with a certain charm. His way of speaking was very spontaneous – the complete opposite of his writing. I never met anyone so polite. But he could be very violent. Everything he did was logical, based on the fact that he was very sensitive and could be hurt by the slightest thing.' When she packed his suitcase for him she knew he would fly into an inexplicable rage if things were not placed exactly as he wanted them to be.

In the fifteen years from 1890 Satie earned his living as a cabaret pianist, which he considered a lowering occupation, and as a composer of music-hall songs and incidental music. Money was a perennial problem; when he had some, which was not often, he was liable to spend it extravagantly. On one occasion he bought seven identical grey corduroy suits, with hats to match, that he wore on all occasions. This led to him being known as the 'velvet gentleman'. Half-way through this period he decided to move away from Montmartre, which was losing its rural character. In 1898 he packed his belongings into a handcart and moved to the rather sordid southern suburb of Arcueil-Cachan, where he rented a small room which no one else was ever allowed to enter. Satie spent many hours in the company of the local street urchins, enjoying their chatter and enthralling them with stories he made up. 'He was attracted by young children…by youth and purity,' said Madeleine Milhaud. 'He shared their joys and hopes. They made up for a deficiency in his own character. They took him as a kind of mascot and thought he brought them luck.'

Every day Satie walked six miles across Paris to the cabaret in Montmartre; at the stroke of two in the morning he started back, stopping for a few drinks on the way, often walking through the night. His only significant composition during these years is the set *Trois morceaux en forme de poire*, written between 1890 and 1903, and consisting for the most part of arrangements of cabaret melodies. In 1905 he decided that he needed to remedy the inadequate musical education of his youth by enrolling at the newly created Schola Cantorum. For three years he studied counterpoint, fugue and orchestration under the august patrician Vincent d'Indy and his assistant Albert Roussel. He won a diploma for his work, but found it difficult to fuse his new contrapuntal skill into a personal style. In 1906 he replaced his velvet gentleman look with that of a bourgeois functionary: bowler hat, wing collar, black suit, and umbrella. This remained his normal dress for the rest of his life.

The beautiful young artist Valentine Hugo, wife of a grandson of Victor Hugo, knew Satie well in these later years:

He was very sensitive. If there was anything he judged to be an insult, or a want of affection, or an unfair piece of gossip, he'd protest in the strongest, most violent language. When he was angry, he either closed up, looking offended, or else burst into brutal sarcasm. You could say he had the serious, ponderous look of a provincial schoolmaster; serious, because of the pince-nez fixed firmly on his nose and the bowler hat tilted slightly forwards; ponderous because his movements were rather slow. He took small steps, with his rolled-up umbrella on his arm. He didn't gesticulate except when he was cheerful or angry. There was nothing remarkable about his voice. It was well-pitched, rather gentle and slow in serious conversation. When he told jokes it became lower. More theatrical and singing; and when he wasn't happy, it was high and acerbic.

At the beginning of 1911 Satie's fortunes began to improve. First, Ravel played his early sarabandes at a concert of the Société Musicale Indépendante, and then Debussy, who had orchestrated his *Gymnopedie*, conducted a performance of this work which was received enthusiastically. Other performances of Satie's work followed, including his recent composition *Quatre préludes flasques*. This attention meant that publishers suddenly began to demand his music. Several of his old compositions were brought out and printed, and he quickly responded with a whole series of humorous piano pieces, with eccentric titles and bizarre commentaries. As his biographer A.N. Gillmor (1988) explains:

> His refusal to commit himself, which in practical matters was a drawback, emerged as one of the great strengths in the artist. He was able to stand back and coolly appraise. Accepted enthusiasms passed him by. Reactions hallowed by unthinking custom were foreign to him. His gaze was cool and fresh. He looked at music anew and put a bomb under it. The incongruous verbal decoration he gave to his derisive piano pieces, the musical techniques of parody and satire, were a healthy counterblast to romantic excess. Having emphasised in this way the absurdities of an outdated style no longer capable of useful exploitation, he evolved an idiom to replace it.

Satie's rise to fame after the war was largely due to young Jean Cocteau, who attended a performance Satie gave of the *Trois morceaux* in 1915. Cocteau used his entrée in elite and wealthy circles to win commissions for Satie, he persuaded virtuosos to perform his work, he wrote and lectured about Satie, and he contributed introductory notes and talks at concert performances. Most important of all he collaborated with Satie in the Diagilev–Massine–Picasso ballet *Parade*.

The opening of *Parade* in May 1917 established Satie's fame once and for all. The critics were out in force and Satie made the mistake of sending an insulting postcard to one who had written a particularly hostile review. He was sued for slander and, after a trial that amounted to an attack on modern art by traditionalists, he was given an eight-day prison sentence and a heavy fine. On appeal the sentence was suspended and the Princesse de Polignac paid the fine, which would have ruined Satie. He emerged from the ordeal as something of a hero to the avant-garde: a group of young composers formed around him which was initially called *Les Nouveaux Jeunes*, later *Les Six*.

Meanwhile, early in 1917 or possibly even before, Satie started work on what is often considered his masterpiece, the cantata *Socrate*. He prepared the text by drastically pruning a rather inferior translation of Plato's *Phaedo*. He was intent from the outset on writing a work that 'should be white and pure like antiquity'. The result was a creation in which his restricted technique came into perfect focus and balance. It was not publicly performed until 1920, but after a private hearing in mid-1919 Igor Stravinsky is said to have remarked: 'French music is Bizet, Chabrier and Satie.' Satie was now enjoying fame and success and the social life they brought. He began to move in high society and enjoyed shocking its members with his Bolshevist views. In 1920 there were two festivals of his music, and in this final creative period his output was far more varied than before. With Milhaud he produced *musique d'ammeublement* (background music), to be played during the intervals in a concert. He also wrote songs, piano music and ballet scores, culminating, in 1924, in *Mercure* (Massin and Picasso) and *Relâche* (designed by Picabia with a filmed entracte by René Clair). Both achieved notoriety.

In 1923, prompted by Milhaud, another group of young composers formed around him. They took the title *l'Ecole d'Arcueil*. But Satie's
health was beginning to deteriorate, through cirrhosis of the liver; for
many years he had been a heavy drinker. He lost what had once been a
prodigious appetite. He became more and more unsociable, and
whenever he went to Paris for a visit he would sit for hours silently in
front of the fire in his hat and coat, with the inevitable umbrella. His
friends set him up in hotels, to spare him the journey to Arcueil and
back. Eventually he had to move to hospital and on 1 July 1925 he
died of liver sclerosis. When his brother Conrad went to Arcueil with
Milhaud and finally entered the room that had been the composer's
home for nearly thirty years they were astounded by its squalor. They
found a bed, chair and table, a half-empty cupboard with the velvet
suits piled on top, an old unused piano whose pedals worked by string,
but little else apart from his manuscript notebooks, dating back to the
1890s, and a large quantity of documents. Most of the latter were
destroyed in a fire, but thanks to Milhaud the music was saved.

The following description must date from relatively late in Satie's
life:

> A short greying goatee, rather thick lips, twisted into a teasing
> smile which could at times be cruel; a sensual, greedy nose. The
> expression of his eyes, hidden behind a pince-nez, could change
> at a moment's notice from gentle to teasing to furious…his face,
> crowned by a strangely pointed skull, was quite beautiful, enig-
> matic and ever-changing…his dress was conventional: he often
> wore a dark grey jacket and a black coat with collar turned up.
> With his umbrella and bowler hat he resembled a quiet school-
> teacher. Although a bohemian he looked very dignified, almost
> ceremonious. A soft, deep voice, unhurriedly familiar and
> friendly, transformed his words into mysterious confidences. He
> was seized with unexpected bursts of laughter, which he would
> stifle with his hand. He walked slowly, taking small steps, his
> umbrella held tight under his arm. When walking he would
> stop, bend one knee a little, adjust his pince-nez and place his
> fist on his hip. Then he would take off once more, with small
> deliberate steps. None of his friends could keep up with him on
> his long nightly walks. He hated the sun…his odd character, his

fits of melancholy, drove him out of doors in the most terrible weather…his conversation was extremely entertaining. Very talkative, he would watch the person to whom he was speaking, through the corner of his eye, judging the effect of his jokes. In the company of a few close friends, he would be truly delightful. Smoking innumerable cigars, he would discourse at great length on any subject with extraordinary lucidity. (Orledge 1995)

Satie's sister Olga said, 'My brother was always difficult to understand: it doesn't seem that he was ever perfectly normal.' One of his friends remarked, 'I doubt whether anybody was entrusted with the favour of a heartfelt outburst from him, whether he ever stopped being witty, precise, a joker. I doubt whether anyone found warmth in Satie's company.' Like most people who are used to suffering in silence he was easily upset and employed jokes as camouflage for his heightened sensitivity. He stuck obstinately to his own opinions. Satie sometimes adopted an exaggerated degree of politeness. He spoke slowly, in a low voice, with a sort of intentness, speaking very softly, hardly opening his mouth, but he delivered each word in an inimitable, precise way. He never washed but cleaned himself with pumice stone instead. His handwriting was absolutely perfect, but it could take him twenty minutes to write a brief *pneumatique*.

Fitzgerald (2005) observes that Satie is a good example of how the 'detachment' of a person with Asperger's syndrome can bear new and interesting fruit. When we look into the family history, to see where the disorder might have come from, our attention is caught by his father's brother Adrien, the black sheep of the family. Known as Sea-Bird, the uncle owned a superbly decorated carriage that nobody dared enter, in case they damaged it. He also had a magnificent boat built, which on rare occasions was put out to sea for a short outing before returning for another long spell in harbour. In childhood Eric saw a lot of this eccentric uncle and felt strangely drawn towards him.

Acknowledgment

The principal sources of information in this chapter are Fitzgerald (2005), Gillmor (1988), Harding (1975) and Orledge (1995).

CHAPTER TEN

Bertrand Russell
(1872–1970)

There must be something wrong about me, as I seem always to be hurting the people I am fondest of, and quite inadvertently. (Bertrand Russell)

According to Fitzgerald and Lyons (2003), Bertrand Russell very closely resembled those individuals who suffer from the personality abnormality of autistic psychopathy as originally described by Asperger. In his case Asperger's syndrome was not a hindrance to the major intellectual achievements in his life. The core symptoms of isolation and loneliness were present throughout his life, as were his emotional detachment and solitary and single-minded pursuit of special interests. Russell himself said: 'I am quite indifferent to the mass of human beings and I live mostly for myself... I care for very few people and have several enemies – for three at least whose pain is delightful to me. I often wish to give pain and when I do I find it pleasant' (Monk 1996).

The mathematician and philosopher Bertrand Russell was born in a Welsh country house on 18 May 1872. In his autobiography he described his mother, a member of the aristocratic and highly intellectual Stanley family, as vigorous, lively, witty, serious, original and fearless, whereas his father, who bore the courtesy title of Lord Amberley, was rather philosophical, studious, morose and priggish. Amberley's father, Bertrand's paternal grandfather, was the great

Liberal reformer Lord John Russell, a younger son of the sixth Duke of Bedford. Twice prime minister under Queen Victoria, he was created Earl Russell and Viscount Amberley, and rewarded with the tenancy of Pembroke Lodge in Richmond Park, where his authoritarian second wife, a Scottish Presbyterian, imposed a Spartan regime on their household. Although a member of the greatest Whig family in the land, Lord Amberley's own political career was brief and unsuccessful; it was said that his manner of public speaking was atrocious, lacking in gesture and intonation. The Russells had a reputation for being cold and abnormally shy.

At the age of two Bertrand and his elder brother Frank lost both their mother and their only sister from diphtheria; only eighteen months later their father also died, and the next year their father's brother William developed schizophrenia. After this series of misfortunes the boys' paternal grandparents took responsibility for their upbringing. Later, in his writings about education, Bertrand often referred to his own childhood, hoping to warn others against what he remembered as unsatisfactory, but he did not describe it as unhappy. His elder brother Frank soon rebelled against the stuffy and morbid atmosphere of Pembroke Lodge; he was sent away to be educated, first at Winchester and then Oxford. Bertrand, however, was educated at home. Later he said that throughout the great part of his childhood:

> the most important hours of my day were those that I spent alone in the garden, and the most vivid part of my experience was solitary. I seldom mentioned my more serious thoughts to others and when I did I regretted it...throughout my childhood I had an increasing sense of loneliness, and of despair of ever meeting anyone with whom I could talk. (Russell 1967)

He learned to hide his thoughts and his feelings. He was taught that sex is wicked and there were allusions to unmentionable events in the lives of his parents. By the age of fourteen his beliefs were so different from those of his grandparents that 'I found living at home only endurable at the cost of complete silence about everything that interested me'.

His grandmother, he recalled, 'had a puritan dislike of vitality and of many innocent forms of enjoyment, she never for a moment doubted her own rightness'. Nevertheless he was devoted to her. An independent-minded lady, she had a strict sense of moral and social duty. She was a defender of social justice, especially the cause of Irish Home Rule, and loved intellectual sparring, coaching her young grandson in the obligations of a liberal reformer. Her social circle included many of the literary and political figures of Victorian England. Russell also benefited from meeting a very remarkable collection of independent and often formidable female relatives of his late mother, who helped to develop his gifts for entertaining and scintillating in company.

In preparation for university Russell was sent to a crammer, where he experienced some rough teasing and bullying from the other boys. His hatred and aggression for one in particular were displayed on one occasion when 'in an excess of fury I got my hands on his throat and started to strangle him. I intended to kill him but when he started to go livid I relented. I do not think he knew that I intended murder.' In 1890 Russell entered Trinity College, Cambridge, on a minor scholarship, to read mathematics. He was soon recognised to be exceptionally able, but when he first arrived he was shy and awkward, very lonely and deeply unhappy. The situation improved when he was elected to the elite Cambridge society known as The Apostles, which played an important part in the early stages of his career. After notable success in the Tripos examinations he was awarded a six-year Prize Fellowship on the strength of an essay on the philosophical foundations of non-Euclidean geometry. But by this time his interests were moving away from mathematics towards philosophy, especially the writings of the great seventeenth-century rationalists Descartes, Spinoza and Leibniz. Incidentally, Fitzgerald (2001) has suggested Spinoza as another Asperger possible.

Russell's first marriage was to Alys Pearsall Smith. When they went to the United States for a short while, after their honeymoon, he amused himself by flirting with various uninhibited young women. Nevertheless, at first the marriage seemed to be working well. One of the most perceptive descriptions of Russell at this stage in his life is to be found in the diaries of the early socialist Beatrice Webb:

> Bertrand is a slight dark-haired man, with prominent forehead, bright eyes, strong features except for a retreating chin, nervous hands and alert quick movements. In manner and dress and outward bearing he is most carefully trimmed, conventionally correct and punctiliously polite, and in speech he has an almost affectedly clear enunciation of words and preciseness of expression. In morals he is a puritan; in personal habits almost an ascetic, except that he lives for efficiency and therefore expects to be kept in the best possible physical condition. But intellectually he is audacious – an iconoclast, detesting religions or social convention, suspecting sentiment, believing only in the 'order of thought' and the order of things, in logic and in science. He indulges in the wildest paradox and in the broadest jokes, the latter always too abstrusely intellectual in their form to be vulgarly coarse. He is a delightful talker, especially in general conversation, when the intervention of other minds prevents him from tearing his subject to pieces with fine chopping logic. What he lacks is sympathy and tolerance for other people. (Webb 1948)

This was written in 1901, by which time Russell had become a protégé of the Cambridge philosopher Alfred North Whitehead. He had fallen in love with Whitehead's wife Evelyn, the first of a series of married women with whom he had affairs. Russell came to realise that he no longer loved Alys and told her so in a most callous fashion, placing all the blame on her, and leaving her heartbroken. Beatrice Webb tried to console Alys but, as she wrote:

> Bertrand Russell's nature is pathetic in its absoluteness: faith in absolute logic, absolute ethic, absolute beauty, and all of the most refined and rarefied type. His abstract and revolutionary methods of thought and the uncompromising way in which he applies these frightens me for his future and the future of those who love him or whom he loves. Compromise, mitigation, mixed motive, phases of health of body and mind, qualified statements, uncertain feelings all seem unknown to him. A proposition must be either true or false, a character good or bad, a person loving or unloving, true speaking or lying. And in this last year he has grown up quite suddenly from an intellectual boy into a masterful man struggling painfully with his own nature and various notions of duty and obligation. (Webb 1948)

Russell consoled himself with his mathematics; as he told a friend, it was 'a haven of peace without which I don't know how I should get on'. He looked to mathematics to provide the perfection that he had failed to find in the transient world of human relations.

Russell was developing his ideas about mathematical logic and the foundations of mathematics, where he was strongly influenced by the works of Georg Cantor and Giuseppe Peano. The outcome was the monumental *Principia Mathematica* that he wrote in collaboration with Whitehead. This led to his election to the Royal Society in 1908; later his stature as a mathematician was recognised by the award of the Sylvester Medal. However, once he discovered that his contributions to the subject had been largely anticipated in the work of Gottlob Frege, Russell turned his attention towards philosophy.

In 1912, a young Austrian named Ludwig Wittgenstein arrived in Cambridge to study under Russell, on the recommendation of Frege.

Wittgenstein's academic status at Cambridge was at first informal, but after two years he became an Advanced Student, with Russell as his supervisor (there was no degree of PhD at Cambridge until after the First World War). They spent a great deal of time together, with Wittgenstein increasingly the dominant partner. Russell was impressed by the depth of Wittgenstein's thought and his intellectual passion, but he found the young man argumentative, obstinate and perverse. For example, Wittgenstein called on him late one evening and said that he was going to commit suicide as soon as he left, but became irritated when Russell tried to talk him out of it. Then the young Austrian paced up and down for hours in agitated silence while Russell was longing to go to bed. More about their relationship will be found in the profile of Wittgenstein in Chapter 14.

Bertrand and Alys were still living together, on and off, in a house they had built in Bagley Wood, on the outskirts of Oxford, close to the home of Alys's mother. Russell remained infatuated with Evelyn Whitehead, until in 1911 her place was taken by Lady Ottoline Morrell, whose country house was nearby. Russell's liaison with Lady Ottoline lasted until her death in 1938. A formidable woman with a great capacity for enjoyment, she collected artistic and intellectual admirers. Her complaisant husband Philip, a shy and insecure Oxford solicitor, was a Liberal back-bencher in parliament. Russell also stood for parliament in a by-election, advocating votes for women, but it was a safe Tory seat and he knew he had no chance of being elected. Many years later he gained a seat in the House of Lords when he succeeded to the earldom after the death of his elder brother.

For hundreds of years the Morrells had owned land in the village of Garsington, a few miles east of Oxford. When the manor house came on the market Philip bought it. After they moved there in 1915 Lady Ottoline made Garsington Manor a centre of hospitality for favoured Oxford undergraduates and for Londoners such as Lytton Strachey and Virginia Woolf. Most of the guests at her house parties were younger than Russell, but he was often present and became an honorary member of the Bloomsbury group. Some of the young men were offered work on the farm as an alternative to military service.

In 1911 Russell had left Alys altogether and returned to Cambridge, where he had been appointed to a special lectureship at Trinity, with the expectation that it might lead to a fellowship. The next year he made the first of several lecture tours in the United States starting with a visit to Harvard, where he was treated as a celebrity. By this time the First World War was imminent. Although no pacifist, Russell was strongly opposed to Britain's participation, and shocked by the militarism of most of the British public. Later, when conscription was introduced, he was prominent in the campaign against the way conscientious objectors were being treated. He was charged with disaffecting the troops, found guilty and fined. The College Council of Trinity then deprived Russell of his lectureship, a hugely controversial action. Later he was prosecuted again, this time for writing an article advocating the acceptance of a German peace offer, and was sentenced to six months' imprisonment, which he was allowed to serve under lenient conditions.

We are now almost half-way through the story of Russell's colourful life, and to avoid taking up too much space I will just mention some of the main events of the stormy second half. Left behind by his protégé Wittgenstein in philosophy, as he was by Frege in mathematics, Russell started to concentrate on writing and lecturing about politics and philosophy, at a popular level. By the end of his life he had written thousands of essays and some seventy books on philosophy, social and political theory, the best of them of a quality that earned him the Nobel Prize for literature. He was never afraid of controversy; of the books he wrote in the period between the wars, *Marriage and Morals*, advocating pre-marital sex, achieved particular notoriety.

Let us go back to 1921, when Russell was divorced from Alys, the first of his four wives, so that he could marry the writer Dora Black, the daughter of a senior civil servant. Formerly a fellow of Girton College, Cambridge, she shared his liberal ideas about parenting and education. In 1927 they started a small school, called Beacon Hill, on the Sussex Downs, so that their son Conrad and daughter Katherine might be educated in accordance with their parents' progressive ideas. The plan was to do away with excessive discipline, religious instruction and the tyranny of adults. Dora was responsible for the management of the school while Bertrand raised funds through writing popular books and lecture tours in the United States. Although Russell supported women's suffrage, he believed that women were less intelligent than men and that their main function was to be wives and mothers. Dora, a leading feminist, could not accept this. By 1930 the marriage had lasted nine years; when it ended in acrimony the children, particularly Conrad, became increasingly depressed, disturbed and disillusioned. The divorce proceedings were finalised in 1935; the next year Russell married the much younger Patricia (Peter) Spence, known for her hot temper. She bore him another son, also called Conrad; his son by Dora subsequently became known as John.

When Russell tried to return to academic life, at the end of this period, he found he was regarded as too old to be considered for a suitable position on either side of the Atlantic. In the end he accepted a one-year appointment at the University of Chicago, which was not a success. This was followed by other short-term engagements until 1941, when the eccentric philanthropist Albert C. Barnes, of Philadelphia, appointed him for five years on a generous salary to deliver a series of popular lectures on philosophy. In fact Barnes dismissed Russell after the first year but the nearby college of Bryn Mawr gave him the facilities he needed to write up the lectures as the hugely successful *History of Western Philosophy*. In 1938 he had been joined in America by Peter and baby Conrad; the older children came out a year later, and they all stayed in the United States throughout the Second World War. In 1944, when the war was almost over, Russell wanted to return to Britain. Unexpectedly his old college Trinity offered him a five-year Visiting Fellowship, which he was glad to accept, although dismayed to find that as a philosopher he was distinctly passé. In 1949 he was appointed to the prestigious Order of Merit.

Meanwhile the older children, John and Kate, had grown up. John, after graduating from Harvard, had joined the Royal Navy while Kate had been the top student in her year at Radcliffe. When they returned to Britain they tried to reconcile the divided family, but Russell still hated Dora and the feud continued. In 1952 his third marriage, with

Peter, ended in divorce, and Russell married another American, the New Yorker Edith Branson Finch, the same year. This last marriage was less turbulent than the others, but there were serious problems elsewhere. In 1953 John, his son by Dora, was diagnosed as having schizophrenia and was never able to work again. Dora struggled to care for the unfortunate John while Russell, after an unsuccessful effort to get his son certified (possibly to prevent him succeeding to the earldom), only saw him once more in the rest of his life. John's divorced wife Susan also suffered from a milder form of the same condition and a further battle took place between Russell and Dora over the grandchildren. Later Susan committed suicide.

For most of his life Russell enjoyed excellent health. Still full of vigour as an octogenarian he played a prominent role in the Campaign for Nuclear Disarmament, although more of a figurehead than a leader. In his declining years he increasingly took personally any dissent from his views. He died at the age of ninety-seven on 2 February 1970, at his Merionethshire home in Penrhyndeudrath. He was survived by the last of his four wives and by his three children. John, whose mental condition had improved considerably, succeeded to the earldom and occasionally attended debates in the House of Lords.

On a number of occasions Russell simply walked out of relationships that he felt were dead, due to his lack of empathy, his exploitation, cruelty and maliciousness. His biographer Ray Monk (1996, 2000) concludes that:

> to research the personal aspects of Russell's life is to plough through a long trail of emotional wreckage that includes broken-hearted lovers, embittered ex-wives, a son who felt destroyed by his father, and grandchildren who have preserved throughout their lives a passionate hatred for him.

Monk described Russell as 'a ghost, a quasi-substantial being only partially in contact with the people around him, someone whose impassability has rendered him almost dead of all warmth and emotions'. Alan Ryan, in a review of Monk's biography, commented that:

there is no doubt that Russell made himself and many other people close to him extraordinarily unhappy; there is no doubt that he was frequently cruel and thoughtless in ways that a less self-engrossed person would not have been, and no doubt that he was casually dismissive of less talented people than himself and that the reverse of the coin was a painful degree of self-loathing. (*Times Literary Supplement* 2000)

'Wasted gifts,' said Beatrice Webb.

Acknowledgment

The principal sources of information in this chapter are Brink (1989), Fitzgerald and Lyons (2003), Kreisel (1973), Monk (1996, 2000), Mooregate (1992), Russell (1967, 1968, 1969) and Wood (1987).

CHAPTER ELEVEN

Albert Einstein (1879–1955)

Einstein was a naturally solitary person, who didn't want his weaknesses to show and didn't want to be helped when they did show. (Eugene Wigner 1967)

Like Newton, Einstein needs no introduction. More than anyone else, he was responsible for laying the foundations of modern physics. He realised that each of the separate fields of physics could devour a short working life without having satisfied the hunger for deeper knowledge, but he had an unmatched ability to scent out the paths that led to the depths and to disregard everything else, all the many things that clutter the mind and divert it from the essential. This ability to grasp precisely the particular simple physical situation that could throw light on questions of general principle characterised much of his thinking. The closing decades of the nineteenth century were the period when the long-established goal of physical theory – the mechanistic explanation of all natural phenomena – came under serious scrutiny and was directly challenged. When Einstein started his scientific work at the beginning of the twentieth century it was a time of startling experimental discoveries, but the problems that drew his attention and forced him to produce the boldly original ideas of a new physics had developed gradually and involved the very foundations of the subject.

Baron-Cohen (in James 2003b) writes that:

In the case of Einstein, we can conclude that he did have Asperger's syndrome. There is evidence for the triad of impairments of social relationships, communication, and obsessional and routine-based behaviour across development. Some clinicians might wonder whether a diagnosis of autism (high-functioning) rather than Asperger's syndrome might be more appropriate, because of the mild language delay and reports of educational slowness in childhood. However he did speak by two or three years old, which is regarded as the upper limit of normal language development, and the educational slowness is likely to have been the reflection of his unusual learning style and lack of social conformity, rather than any reflection of cognitive delay.

Albert Einstein was born in the city of Ulm, in the state of Baden-Württemberg, on 14 March 1879. He was the only son of Hermann and Pauline (née Koch); both sides of the family were Jews from the south German region of Swabia. His father Hermann was a gentle, kind but somewhat ineffectual person; his mother the more dominant parent. His father's brother, who lived with the family, was a trained electrical engineer; together they ran a business designing and manufacturing electrical apparatus, such as dynamos. Not long after the birth of Albert the family moved to Munich, the Bavarian capital. A year after that a daughter Maria was born, who resembled her brother in many ways; there were no other children.

Einstein did not speak fluently until he was seven; before that he was prone to emotional outbursts. The family history has a high incidence of autism, dyslexia and food allergies, as well as exceptional gifts. It is widely believed that Einstein himself was dyslexic; he was certainly echolalic, softly repeating to himself what had just been said to him. Also he avoided eye contact. He attended a Catholic primary school before proceeding to the Leopold Gymnasium, a conventional school of good repute. He hated history and geography, but was keen on arithmetic. He disliked sport and gymnastics. His scientific interests were awakened early by a small magnetic compass his father gave him when he was about four; by the algebra he learned from his uncle; and by the books he read, mostly popular science works of the day. A little book on plane Euclidean geometry that he studied at the age of twelve made a deep impression – he described it as the holy booklet. We have some details of Einstein's childhood from his son Hans Albert:

> He was a very well-behaved child. He was shy, lonely and with-drawn from the world even then. He was even considered backward by his teachers. He told me that his teachers reported to his father that he was mentally slow, unsociable and adrift forever in his foolish dreams. (Brian 1996)

Very early Einstein set himself the task of establishing himself as an entirely separate entity, influenced as little as possible by other people. In school he did not revolt, he simply ignored authority. His parents, although Jewish, were largely indifferent to religion. Einstein, while still a schoolboy, deliberately emphasised his Jewish origin and went through a period of religious fervour which he later described as his 'first attempt to liberate myself from purely personal links'. When the family business failed in 1894 after an over-ambitious attempt to compete with much stronger firms, the rest of the family moved from Munich to Pavia in Lombardy, leaving the fifteen-year-old Einstein in the care of distant relatives. The intention was to enable him to continue his education, but he felt abandoned. He found the authoritarian Leopold Gymnasium, with its emphasis on classics, increasingly unbearable. Before long he left, ostensibly on medical grounds, but perhaps more to avoid liability for military service, and joined the family in Pavia. One of his first actions was to renounce his German citizenship, thereby becoming stateless. After spending most of a year enjoying life in Italy he resumed his education, but the family business was again failing and he could expect no financial support from his parents. To see him through school and university an aunt in Genoa made him a monthly allowance, but after that he would need to support himself.

Einstein's aim was to enter the Zurich Polytechnic Institute (later merged with the university) but to do so he had to pass the entrance examination. After one unsuccessful attempt, due to a poor performance in non-scientific subjects, he was advised to complete his school education first. Accordingly, he spent a year at the Gymnasium in the Swiss town of Aarau, where the liberal regime was influenced by

Pestalozzi. His teachers thought him lazy and were unimpressed, but in physics and mathematics he already knew a great deal more than his classmates.

Some people process visual information better than that given in purely spoken form. This is a handicap at school, where so much teaching is verbal rather than visual. Einstein was an extreme example; he explained that:

> Thoughts do not come in any verbal formulation. I rarely think in words at all. A thought comes and I try to explain it in words afterwards. Words and language, whether written or spoken, do not seem to play any part in my thought processes. The psychological entities that serve as building blocks for my thought are certain signs or images, more or less clear, that I can reproduce or recombine at will. (Wertheimer 1959)

Later in life he proved to be a confusing lecturer, giving specific examples of something followed by seemingly unrelated general principles. Sometimes he would lose his train of thought while writing on the blackboard. A few minutes later he would emerge from a trance and go on to something different.

By the time Einstein gained the necessary certificate and was admitted to the Polytechnic Institute his main interests centred on theoretical physics. He avoided regular classes and spent most of his time studying the classical texts of the subject, especially the works of Clerk Maxwell. Einstein was impressed by both the successes and failures of the old physics, and was attracted to what he later called the 'revolutionary' ideas of Maxwell's field theory of electromagnetism. After graduation he became a Swiss citizen; as a result he again became liable for military service, but was rejected on medical grounds. For two years he sought school teaching posts but was unable to obtain regular employment. While supporting himself by occasional tutoring and substitute teaching, he published several scientific papers. Then, in 1902, he was appointed an expert examiner at the Swiss patent office in Berne. The seven years Einstein spent there, examining applications for patents in electro-technology, were the years in which he laid the foundations of large parts of twentieth-century physics. He liked the fact that his official work, which only occupied part of the day, was entirely separate from his scientific work, so that he could pursue that freely and independently, and he often recommended this arrangement to others later on.

At this stage in his life Einstein stood about five and a half feet tall. His features were regular, with warm brown eyes, a mass of jet-black hair and a slightly raffish moustache. 'I'm not much with people,' he would say, but he was physically attractive to women and had a number of affairs. In 1903, against strong opposition from his mother (his father had died the previous year), Einstein married Mileva Maric, a Serbian science student from the university, more or less his contemporary academically, although five years senior in age. Their two sons were born in Switzerland, Hans Albert in 1904 and Eduard in 1910. A previous child Lieserl was born at the home of Mileva's parents and given for adoption; it is not known what became of her. Hans Albert emigrated to the United States before the Second World War and became professor of hydraulic engineering at the University of California; for various reasons he felt bitter towards his father. Eduard was a gifted child; as a young man his resemblance to his father was said to be 'almost frightening'. He suffered from paranoid schizophrenia, and after he was institutionalised his father had nothing more to do with him.

All observers agree that Einstein had a passion for music, as a way of experiencing and expressing emotion that is impersonal. He was an enthusiastic violinist; Mozart, Bach and Schubert were his favourite composers. When he was world famous as a physicist he is reported to have said that music was as important to him as physics: 'it is a way for me to be independent of people'; on another occasion he described it as the most important thing in his life. Photographs of him playing the violin show a different Einstein from the more familiar images.

In 1905, one marvellous year, Einstein produced three masterly papers on three different subjects that revolutionised the way scientists regarded the nature of space, time and matter. These papers dealt with the nature of the Brownian motion, the quantum nature of electromagnetic radiation and the special theory of relativity. Einstein considered the second paper, on the light quantum, or photon, as the most important, and it was for this that he was awarded the Nobel prize, but it was relativity that caught the popular imagination. Max Wertheimer (1959) has placed on record the steps which led Einstein to this fundamental theory. It took a few years for Einstein's research to receive recognition. When he submitted the relativity paper to support his application to become *Privatdozent* (tutor) at the University of Berne, it was rejected, although he was invited to give some lectures. His academic career did not really get started until three years later when he was appointed associate professor at Zurich University; two years after that he became full professor at the German University in Prague, and then returned to Zurich as full professor at the Polytechnic Institute the following year. Finally, in the spring of 1914, Einstein was persuaded to move to the Berlin Academy, free to lecture at the university or not as he chose, and appointed director of the new Kaiser Wilhelm Institute of Physics. He had mixed feelings about the move, partly because he disliked the Prussian lifestyle and partly because in physics he felt he would be expected to go on producing one successful theory after another. As it turned out, however, he found the cultural atmosphere in the German capital very stimulating.

However, while Einstein's scientific work was flourishing, his marriage had been under strain for some years. His wife Mileva and their two sons followed him to Berlin but before long they returned to Zurich, the city which remained Mileva's home for the rest of her life. Legal separation and finally divorce followed soon after the end of the war. Earlier, when Einstein became ill and was bedridden for some months, he was nursed back to health by his cousin and childhood friend Elsa Löwenthal, a widow with two daughters; when the divorce came through, in which violence towards Mileva and adultery with Elsa were cited, they got married. She was three years his senior, totally ignorant of science, but more maternal and protective towards him than Mileva had been. Einstein gradually lost interest in her.

Einstein's chief outdoor recreation was sailing a dinghy on the numerous lakes formed by the River Havel around Berlin. He was very skilful at manipulating his little boat, enjoying the gliding motion and the quiet mind-soothing scenery. He could be seen almost every day out sailing, but he lacked a mooring for the boat. As the date of his fiftieth birthday approached the municipality conceived the plan of giving its most distinguished citizen a birthday present: a house beside the lakes that would give him quiet and direct access to the water. Unfortunately the project became so entangled in politics that Einstein rejected the idea and simply built a lakeside house for himself.

By this time the anti-Semitic Nazi party was in power and Einstein was one of their prime targets. He left Germany, after resigning from the Berlin Academy and other academies of which he was a member, and gave up German citizenship for a second time. He spent some time in Oxford, and some more in Pasadena, not sure where to settle down. In the end he chose the newly founded Institute for Advanced Study in Princeton, the place that became Einstein's home for the remaining twenty-two years of his life. He described it as 'a wonderful piece of earth and at the same time an exceedingly amusing ceremonial back-water of tiny spindle-shanked demigods'. This rather rude comment was reciprocated: Einstein was known as 'old stone-face'. His *heldenzeit* had lasted a good twenty years, but well before he left Europe his best days were over. When he first arrived he was happy and gregarious, but he became increasingly preoccupied with world affairs. Scientifically the Princeton years were much less fruitful than what came before. To the end of his life he remained faithful to his unified field theory, and took no interest in the ideas of the young physicists who were working in the same building as he was.

When Einstein was in his prime one of his colleagues, after observing him at close quarters, concluded that the towering intellect was combined with a pathetic naivety in the ordinary affairs of life. In later years the shy genius impressed everyone who met him by his gentleness and wisdom, but as he explained:

> I do not socialize because social encounters would distract me from my work and I really only live for that, and it would shorten even further my very limited lifespan. I do not have any close friends here as I had in my youth or later in Berlin with whom I could talk and unburden myself. That may be due to my age. I often have the feeling that God has forgotten me here. Also

> my standard of decent behaviour has risen as I grew older: I
> cannot be sociable with people whose fame has gone to their
> heads. (Pais 1982)

On one occasion he said that really his only friend in Princeton was
the logician Kurt Gödel, who used to call for him every morning at 11
o'clock so that, whatever the weather, they could walk together the
mile to Fuld Hall. Gödel, another émigré from central Europe, had his
own version of the theory of relativity, although his reputation rests on
his profound contributions to mathematical logic.

After 1936 when his second wife Elsa died, Einstein was looked
after by his sister Maria, his stepdaughter Margot and his secre-
tary-housekeeper. Maria had come to live with her brother in 1939;
she suffered a stroke in 1946, after which she was bedridden, and died
in 1951. Einstein retired from the Institute for Advanced Study in
1945 and became almost a recluse, trying to avoid the endless stream
of people who wanted to see him about something, or just to see him.
He suffered much harassment by press photographers; no other scientist has become so well known to the public in appearance. He was
generally quite a merry person, with a ribald sense of humour and a
loud guffaw; on one occasion he put out his tongue to express his
annoyance and that photograph has been endlessly reproduced.
Around Princeton he could often be seen at the local cinema – he was
particularly fond of cowboy films. He never learned to drive a car, but
used to sail a dinghy on Lake Carnegie. Otherwise he stayed peace-
fully at home in number 112 Mercer Street, a Colonial-style house no
different from others in the neighbourhood.

At the age of sixty-seven Einstein made some notes for an autobiography, but he felt it was rather like writing his own obituary. For
many years he had experienced recurrent health problems, including
anaemia and digestive attacks, and he also suffered from an enlarged
heart. One day, when he was seventy-six, he was drafting a speech on
the tensions between Israel and Egypt when he became seriously ill.
He died a few days later, on 18 April 1955, due to a haemorrhage after
a large aneurysm of the abdominal aorta burst. One of his last acts was
to sign a plea, initiated by Russell, for the renunciation of nuclear

weapons. He left his brain for use in research, his body for cremation, and all his scientific and other papers to the Weizmann Institute in Jerusalem.

Einstein never identified with any particular country, living and working in various places, and although he had quite a few individual collaborators, he never set out to create a research school in any sense. In his own words:

> I have never belonged wholeheartedly to any country or state, to my circle of friends, or even to my own family. These ties have always been accompanied by a vague aloofness, and the wish to withdraw into myself increases with the years. Such isolation is sometimes bitter, but I do not regret being cut off from the understanding and sympathy of other men. I lose something by it, to be sure, but I am compensated for it by being rendered independent of the customs, opinions and prejudices of others, and am not tempted to rest my peace of mind on such shifting foundations. (James 2003a)

Acknowledgment

The biographical information in this chapter is based on James (2003a). The other principal sources of information in this chapter are Brian (1996), Fitzgerald (2000), Fölsing (1997), French (1979), Highfield and Carter (1993), Hoffman with Dukas (1972), Overbye (2003), Pais (1982), Sowell (2001) and Vallentin (1954).

CHAPTER TWELVE

Béla Bartók
(1881–1945)

While Bartók played, it was as if all music lived in him, and the listener was impressed by his strong individuality, but when he ceased playing he returned to the remotest depths of some cavern, from which he could be drawn only by force. (Oscar Brie)

The contribution of Hungarians to the arts and sciences has been quite remarkable. In the case of music, the composer Béla Bartók is outstanding. Biographers have described Bartók as self-contained, introspective and showing in his writings a meticulous adherence to facts. There are references to him being socially awkward, a man of limited conversation, and possessing a probing combative nature. There is general agreement that he was a hard person to be with; few could feel really comfortable in his presence. We are told that he was 'possessed of a fanatical will and pitiless severity', that he was almost painfully shy, incurably nervous and reservedly polite. Except at the keyboard, his movements often seemed to be 'hesitating and somewhat stiff', suggestive of motor clumsiness. As for peculiarities of speech and language, everyone agreed that Bartók was remarkably laconic. The intonation of his speaking voice was said to be 'exceedingly grey and monotonous'. He rarely emphasised a particular word; his words flowed out completely evenly. His voice was said to be 'excessively deep, disciplined and serene', his speech 'unusually clear, plain and at the same time, restrained, matter-of-fact and concentrated'. His letters were always written in a small, clear script that looked as if every word had been put down slowly and deliberately. Neither time nor space was ever wasted in courtesies, on how-do-you-dos, on anything personal that had no connection with the subject of his message. Gillberg (2002) and Sula Wolff (1995) have both said they believe that he suffered from some disorder in the autistic spectrum. Fitzgerald (2000a) also discusses Bartók's case and concludes that there is evidence to support a diagnosis of pervasive developmental disorder.

Bartók was born in an agricultural district of what was then Hungary on 25 March 1881. When the district was taken into Romania after the First World War, his birthplace was renamed Sanmiclusulmare. His father, also named Béla, was a man of many enthusiasms, music among them. He died of Addison's disease when his son was only eight years old. Writing of him later, Bartók described his father as a gifted musician who not only played the piano, and learned to play the cello so that he might play in a little amateur orchestra, but also composed dance pieces. Bartók's mother Paula (née Voit) was also a keen amateur musician; she had given birth to a daughter Erzsebet in 1885. Bartók's attachment to his mother was enormously strong and he remained utterly devoted to her until her death in 1939.

Bartók's childhood was beset by illness. He was vaccinated against smallpox at the age of three months, and suffered for a number of years from eczema. Other sickness, including pneumonia, delayed him in learning to walk, and he was over two years old before he began to talk; when he did so, he spoke in complete sentences right away. A bronchial condition developed when he was five; then spinal curvature was diagnosed and the boy was subject to drastic treatment; later another physician was consulted and decided that this was quite unnecessary. Bartók was a serious, quiet child, prevented by the state of his health from playing with other children; instead he spent a great deal of time listening to his mother's songs and stories.

Bartók started school at the age of six. He had already displayed a strong inclination towards music at home, and his musical education began early. Lessons were interrupted by further illness, and it was not until he was seven that he was found to possess absolute pitch. In 1888, shortly after his father died, the family began a series of removals that brought them in 1894 to a permanent home in Pozsony (Bratislava today). Located on the Danube between Vienna and Budapest, the cosmopolitan town had a long cultural tradition, especially in music; only the capital enjoyed more orchestral concerts and opera. His mother helped to pay for her son's education through giving piano lessons as well as earning a living as a schoolteacher, while her sister Irma took care of the house. Although the boy did not shine at the gymnasium, he was already making his mark as a pianist and beginning to perform compositions of his own. He was also interested in entomology and loved collecting insects. Having been isolated from other children in his early years, he found it difficult to form friendships with them later on, and disliked their noisy games and quarrels. They accepted his seriousness, liked his modesty, and benefited from his help with their lessons. Ignored by his teachers, he read a great deal. Language held a fascination for him. Hungary under the Habsburgs was bilingual: both Magyar and German were necessities. He learned Latin with a tutor, took some lessons in Italian and Spanish, studied English and French, and later, when he was collecting folk music, he needed Slovak and Romanian, and so he also learned to speak these languages.

He was now at the stage where a few years at a leading conservatoire would have been appropriate to complete his musical education. Vienna would have been the obvious choice for this, but instead Bartók followed his friend Erno Dohnanyi by going to Budapest. Again illness struck, bronchial infections, then pneumonia, but Bartók's musical career made good progress at the Royal Academy of Music, more as pianist than composer. Wagner and Liszt were popular in Hungary, and he studied their work, but after hearing *Also Sprach Zarathustra*, he was carried away by enthusiasm for Richard Strauss's music and began to follow his technical style.

During Bartók's final years as a student there was a revival of Hungarian nationalism, suppressed since the catastrophic uprising in

1848–49. In the concert hall, however, the programmes were still dominated by Austrian and German compositions; what passed for Hungarian music was merely gypsy music. The existence of a strong Magyar musical tradition among the peasantry was only just becoming recognised. With his friend Zoltan Kodaly, Bartók began to collect this material and incorporate it into his own work. Almost by chance he discovered the vast reservoir of peasant song in his native country, previously unplumbed and on the brink of disappearance. Together with a few other enthusiasts, he systematically collected and scientifically classified thousands of melodies from Hungary and neighbouring countries; his musico-ethnological publications, both books and periodical articles, have greatly enriched the store of knowledge concerning the Magyar, Romanian, Slovak and other peoples. He also collected examples of traditional handicrafts and peasant artefacts that he always arranged in a particular way.

A recital Bartók gave in Berlin in 1903 was well received: he played works by Schumann, Liszt, Chopin, Dohnanyi and some of his own compositions. He gave another in Manchester the next year; the following year he went to Paris to compete for the Prix Rubinstein, but without success. On the platform he was the picture of self-control but he always disliked performing in public, due to incurable nervousness. Although he had some success as a concert pianist, the way Bartók earned his living for the next thirty years was by teaching the piano at the Academy. In composition the influence of Strauss began to diminish and he developed his own characteristic harsh, violent, untempered style. He was ahead of most of his contemporaries, experimenting with bitonality, dissonant counterpoint and chords in intervals other than thirds. Unfortunately, because of this, he had difficulty in getting his compositions performed.

Bartók seemed attracted by women much younger than himself. His first wife, Marta, had been a pupil of his at the age of fourteen. She was alert, well read, musical and unaffected, qualities he valued highly. By 1909 she was sixteen and they got married. The story is told of how one day she had come to Bartók's home for a lesson, and when it was time for lunch he told his mother 'Marta will stay.' After the meal the lesson went on; presently teacher and pupil went out for a while, returned and continued the lesson until dinner time. When Paula Bartók announced dinner, Bartók again said 'Marta will stay' – and added, 'She is my wife.' Their first child, also named Béla, was born the following year. It gave Bartók great pleasure to see the boy develop, although he showed no musical aptitude.

The First World War ended with the defeat of the Central Powers, the dissolution of the Habsburg empire and in Hungary the short-lived communist government of Béla Kun, with its disastrous effect on the economy. Conditions in Hungary were so bad that Bartók thought of emigrating, but in the end decided to remain. Although confident of the merits of his work, he was not a self-publicist, and began to feel he was being deprived of his due recognition. The problem was that he tended to isolate himself from people who could help him. Absorbed in his own career to the point of rudeness he was often snubbed by those in authority and came to behave as a disgruntled internal exile. Although a dutiful and loving family man, he could not completely accommodate domestic demands, which habitually had to take second place to the task at hand. In combination, this integrity and personal inflexibility caused Bartók's life to be more fraught and less immediately rewarding than it might have been.

There is no shortage of recollections of Bartók, from which we learn that his hazel eyes had a penetrating look, that his hair was white, but his face youthful in appearance. His speech was unusually clear and matter-of-fact, his voice deep and serene. His normal manner was unpretentious and unassuming, but at the piano he seemed like a panther in his movements, his stretchings and sudden starts. He knew well his own mind and self-appointed mission, and saw no virtue in circumlocution or in furthering the polite urbanities of social intercourse. His piano students were sometimes driven to distraction owing to his uncompromising insistence on exactly the right turn of phrase or rhythmic realisation. As some commentators have suggested, his external brittleness functioned like a mask, which with only limited success shielded a naturally shy, super-sensitive yet determined individual from the hurly-burly of the world. Late in 1925 the London music critic Frank Whitaker visited the composer at his home in Budapest and wrote a piece for the *Musical Times* afterwards:

> Physically as well as mentally Bartók presents striking antitheses. His loosely brushed hair is white, though his tanned face is young for his forty-four years. His strong, ruggedly rhythmical music suggests that he is big and powerful, but he is slight and lean, with hands and feet almost as delicate as a woman's...on the platform, at the pianoforte, he whirls tempestuously through his part; in private he is gentleness itself – alert but not aggressive, precise without being pedantic. In his grave old-world courtesy there is not a trace of affectation. One is conscious all the while of his virility, but it is of the kind that burns inwardly – that glitters through the eyes rather than expends itself in gesture, his eyes, indeed, stamp him at once as a remarkable man. They are of a rich golden brown, and he has a habit of opening them wide and slowly tilting back his head as he waits for a question. (Gillies 1990)

One of Bartók's students in the Academy was a young girl, Ditta Pasztory, whose pianistic talents were impressive and whose personal charms were irresistible. For the second time in his life Bartók found himself drawn towards a woman much younger than he was. The result was that his first marriage broke down and was dissolved by divorce; in 1923 he married Ditta. They also had a son, named Peter; unlike Béla, the son by Bartók's first marriage, Peter displayed some aptitude for music.

During the 1920s Bartók was busy making concert tours throughout Western Europe and in the United States, although he still mainly performed in Hungary and neighbouring countries. The decade ended with a concert tour of the Soviet Union. However, much of his time and energy continued to be spent on the collection of folk music; he once went to North Africa for this purpose, but it was more usually in remote areas of the Balkans, especially his native Hungary. Sometimes, without warning, he would vanish for months on these expeditions. In 1934 he was relieved of his piano-teaching responsibilities at the Academy of Music and transferred to the Hungarian Academy of Sciences, where he could devote himself to ethnomusicology. In the next few years he prepared numerous volumes of Hungarian, Romanian and Slovak folk music but could only gain significant international dissemination of a single-volume study of Hungarian folk song. He was very interested to know where the music of the Hungarian peasantry originated, and thought it might have been Turkey, particularly the nomadic tribes that inhabit the south-eastern part of the peninsula between the Taurus Mountains and the Mediterranean Sea, close to the border with Syria. When he visited that area he found confirmation of this, although he was not allowed to hear women singing, and could only talk to the peasants through an interpreter.

Bartók had no love for Germany, and when the Nazis annexed Austria and threatened to spill over into Hungary, he decided it was time to leave. He sent his manuscripts to Switzerland for safe-keeping and signed a contract with the London firm of Boosey and Hawkes that provided him with a regular income in return for publication rights to all his work. He thought of emigrating to Turkey; when this proved impossible, he considered Switzerland. Among his Swiss friends was the young conductor Paul Sacher, founder of the Basler Kammerorchester, which often performed new music. Sacher gave this vivid impression of the composer:

> Whoever met Bartók, thinking of the rhythmic strength of his work, was surprised by his slight delicate figure. He has the outward appearance of a fine-nerved scholar possessed of a fanatical will and pitiless severity, and propelled by an ardent spirit, he affected inaccessibility and was reservedly polite. His being breathed light and brightness, his eyes burned with a noble fire… If in performance an especially hazardous and refractory passage came off well he laughed with boyish glee; and when he was pleased with the successful solution to a problem, he actually beamed. (Gillies 1990)

In the end, however, the Bartóks found refuge in the United States; on a brief preliminary visit, he was offered a temporary appointment at Columbia University, where there was a large collection of Balkan folk music awaiting his expert attention. He returned to Budapest only to join his wife and make preparations for their departure. In the autumn

of 1940 they made their way across southern Europe with some difficulty, and by the end of October were safely in New York.

Columbia University welcomed him with the award of an
honorary degree. The entry of the United States into the war cut off his
income from Hungary, but Hungarian immigrants who had settled in
America provided some financial assistance. The American public were
slow to realise that one of the great composers of the twentieth century
had come to work in their country. Before taking up his appointment
he made a concert tour, but initially the reception given to his own
compositions was not encouraging. Although research in the archives
of the university was congenial, the post he held could not be made
permanent, so Bartók had to start looking elsewhere. Encouraged by
an offer from the University of Washington in Seattle, he began to plan
a whole series of major works, but at the beginning of 1943 his health
broke down. The diagnosis was polycythemia, an increase in the hae-
moglobin concentration of the blood. He was given blood transfu-
sions, and was perhaps the first civilian patient to receive penicillin
injections. Bartók died of leukaemia in New York on 26 September
1945, at the age of sixty-four.

Acknowledgment

The principal sources of information in this chapter are Chalmers (1995), Fitzgerald
(2005), Gillies (1990) and Stevens (1993).

CHAPTER THIRTEEN

Ramanujan
(1887–1920)

His mind was a slave to his genius. (E.H. Neville)

India has given the world some remarkable scientists. Although the mathematician Ramanujan may not be one of the most important, the story of his life is of exceptional interest. Fitzgerald discusses his case in *Autism and Creativity* (2004), and concludes that he is a perfect example of Asperger's syndrome, adding that he also met the criteria for schizoid personality. The indications are his gifts must have come from the mother's side. She had mathematical ability herself and believed that her son's exceptional powers were of divine origin.

Srinivasa Iyengar Ramanujan was born on 22 December 1887 in his mother's hometown of Erode and raised in the city of Kumbakonam in the Tanjore district of the Madras province of India. The family was orthodox Brahman but poor. His father worked as a bookkeeper in a cloth-merchant's establishment. His mother, the dominant parent, came from a line of famous Sanskrit scholars. A shrewd, manipulative, cultured and above all deeply religious woman, she often sang devotional songs with a group at a local temple to supplement the family income. The son remained close to his mother in adulthood and bore a strong resemblance to her physically. His 'very quiet' father had little influence on his upbringing. As a child Ramanujan would take the brass and copper vessels in the house and 'line them up from one wall to the other'. If he did not get what he wanted he would roll on the ground in frustration. While he was still quite young his mother had other children who died in infancy. Much later two more sons were born who lived to manhood, but the young Ramanujan was effectively an only child. He suffered from smallpox when he was two. At the age of three he scarcely spoke at all; his mother was very worried about this.

Ramanujan received all his early education in Kumbakonam, where he studied English at primary school and then attended the town's secondary school where the teaching was in the English language. He preferred his own company and had no interest in sport. His mathematical talents became evident early on; at eleven he was already challenging his mathematics teachers with questions they could not always answer. Seeing his interest in the subject, some college students lent him books. By the time he was thirteen Ramanujan had mastered a popular textbook on trigonometry used by students much older than himself. His classmates described him as 'someone off in the clouds with whom they could scarcely hope to communicate'. In 1904 he graduated from school, winning a special prize in mathematics and a scholarship to attend college.

Shortly before this Ramanujan came across a book called *A Synopsis of Elementary Results in Pure and Applied Mathematics*, written by a British mathematics coach. Without much in the way of explanation, it listed thousands of results, formulae and equations. In Ramanujan this unleashed a passion for mathematics so overwhelming that he studied it to the exclusion of all other subjects. As a result he began failing examinations and his scholarship was revoked. He started proving results that were not in the *Synopsis*, and some of these were completely new to mathematics. He recorded them in a notebook that he showed to people he thought might be interested. A classmate of his described how Ramanujan 'would open his notebooks and explain to me intricate theorems and formulae without the least suspecting that they were beyond my understanding or knowledge'. It was clear that 'once Ramanujan was lost in mathematics, the other person was as good as gone'.

Without a university degree it was very difficult for him to find a suitable job, and for some years Ramanujan was desperately poor, often relying on friends and family for support. Occasionally he would tutor students in mathematics but without great success because he did not keep to the syllabus and the standard methods. In 1909 his mother found a bride for him named Janaki, some ten years his junior. When she was old enough to leave her parents and live with him his mother forbade them to share a bed. Soon after the marriage he left home and travelled to Madras, the principal city of south India, in search of a livelihood; eventually a professor of mathematics named Rao at the prestigious Presidency College, impressed by the work Ramanujan showed him, provided temporary financial support. Later he described how Ramanujan appeared to him at this time:

> A short, uncouth figure, stout, unshaved, not overclean, with one conspicuous feature – shining eyes – walked in with a frayed notebook under his arm. He was miserably poor. He had run away from Kumbakonam to get leisure in Madras to pursue his studies. He never craved for any distinction. He wanted leisure; in other words, that simple food should be provided for him without exertion on his part and that he should be allowed to dream on. He opened his book and began to explain some of his discoveries. I saw quite at once that there was something out of the way; but my knowledge did not permit me to judge whether he was talking sense or nonsense. Suspending judgement I asked him to come over again and he did. And then he had gauged my ignorance and showed me some of his simpler results. These transcended existing books and I had no doubt he was a remarkable man. Then, step by step, he led me to elliptic integrals and hypergeometric series and at last his theory of divergent series not yet announced to the world converted me. I asked him what he wanted. He said he wanted a pittance to live on so that he could pursue his researches. (Kanigel 1991)

In 1912 Ramanujan finally obtained a poorly paid post as an accounts clerk at the Madras Port Trust. When not so occupied he would sit writing on the front porch of his house, his legs pulled in to his body, a large slate pulled across his lap, madly scribbling, seemingly oblivious

to the squeak of the hard slate pencil upon it. For all the noisy activity
in the street, he inhabited an island of serenity. His wife would later
recall how, before going to work in the morning, he worked on mathematics, and how, when he came home in the evening, he also worked
on mathematics. Sometimes he would stay up until dawn, then sleep
for two or three hours before going off to his job. His mathematical
discoveries were beginning to attract the attention of other scholars,
who recognised his abilities and encouraged him to continue research.

Those who knew him in those days described him as friendly and
gregarious, always full of rather childish fun. His lack of social sensitivity conferred on him an innocence and sincerity, a child-like sim-
plicity, so that people could not help but like him. He had a peculiar
stiff gaze; 'The glow in his eyes would captivate us,' said one of his
friends. He walked with his body pitched forward onto his toes. In
appearance he was 'fair and plumpy', according to one of his friends,
with hands like those of a woman. Another referred to his fair complexion, slightly pitted face and dreamy eyes with an absent-minded
look about them. In conversation he would tend to remain silent,
although listening to what was said, but when asked a question he
would speak frankly but briefly.

In 1913 Ramanujan began writing to leading mathematicians in
Cambridge about his discoveries. The first two he approached were
unhelpful; however, the third was G.H. Hardy, perhaps the premier
British mathematician at that time. Something about Ramanujan's
letter, perhaps its very strangeness, intrigued Hardy, and he decided
that it was worth a closer look. Later he would rank it as the most
remarkable he had ever received. Ramanujan, after a single paragraph
of introduction, plunged into formulae and theorems stated without
proofs. Hardy's first reaction was to disregard it as the work of a crank,
filled as it was with wild claims and bizarre theorems without any
proofs being offered in support. When Hardy examined what
Ramanujan sent him he noticed 'wild theorems – theorems such as he
had never seen before, nor imagined'. He asked his mathematical colleague J.E. Littlewood to join him; after three hours of perusal the two
men decided they were dealing with a genius. Hardy then wrote back

to Ramanujan asking for some proofs, but when Ramanujan wrote again it was to provide even more results without proofs. To Hardy, who had reintroduced rigour into the British school of mathematical analysis, the intuitive reasoning of Ramanujan was very frustrating, but of course the young Indian might have been reluctant to disclose his secrets to a stranger.

With Littlewood's support, Hardy decided to try to lure Ramanujan to Cambridge. However, as an orthodox Brahman, Ramanujan explained that he would lose caste by travelling overseas. While Hardy was naturally disappointed, he continued to try to persuade Ramanujan to come to Cambridge. As an interim measure a two-year fellowship was arranged for Ramanujan at the University of Madras. Eventually, with the help of Hardy's colleague E.H. Neville, who was visiting Madras in 1914, the objections to Hardy's plan were overcome. Before leaving India Ramanujan had been advised, quite wrongly, that he would need to wear Western clothes and conform in other ways that caused him much unhappiness. In Cambridge, under the guidance of Hardy and Littlewood, especially Hardy, Ramanujan developed rapidly. However, he found living in college had its problems. 'Till now I did not feel comfortable and I would often think why I had come here,' he wrote soon after arrival. Ramanujan was very particular about food, for religious reasons, and insisted on preparing his own meals; he had left his wife behind in India, where her mother-in-law was ill-treating her. This was the main problem, but there were others: he complained of being cold in bed, until it was suggested he try sleeping under the bedclothes rather than on top of them.

At Cambridge he would work for up to thirty hours at a time. He was taunted by students because of his shyness; he was said to be 'not particularly attuned to interpersonal nuance'. When Indian visitors called on him they were most impressed by his mysticism. One of them wrote:

> I had many an occasion to hear from his visitors who were evidently taken by surprise by the unimposing figure of the great genius and the scantily supplied shelves. 'Are you the great

mathematician?' Naturally the very prime object of the query used to shrink further into his chair on such occasions. But after the visitor left, Ramanujan used to ask me 'Can you suggest the appropriate reply to the question and describe the dramatic pose to be assumed in giving that reply?' (James 2002)

Ramanujan was extremely sensitive, especially to the slightest hint of public humiliation. Even before he left India he had a reputation for sudden 'disappearances'. On one occasion, in 1916, he was entertaining some Indian friends at his apartment in Cambridge. He was proud of his skill in cooking. His guests had several servings of the South Indian food he had prepared and, after they expressed their appreciation, he offered them yet more. When the ladies present politely declined he felt so ashamed that he got up without a word, called a taxi, and disappeared for a week to Oxford. Such disappearances, in the wake of an intolerable blow to their self-esteem, are not unusual in people with Asperger's.

It was inevitable that a large portion of the results in Ramanujan's notebooks consisted of rediscoveries; he had never had any systematic training or access to a good library. To quote Hardy:

> What is to be done in the way of teaching him modern mathematics? The limitations of his knowledge were as startling as its profundity. He had only the vaguest idea of complex analysis. Most of the theorems in his notebooks were not proved but only made to seem plausible. His ideas of what constituted a mathematical proof were of the most shadowy description. Because he tended to collapse many steps in his mathematical work it was very difficult for other people to work out how he got his results. He had a very deep mathematical insight and a knack for manipulating formulas, a delight in mathematical form for its own sake. (Hardy, cited in James 2002)

According to Hardy, Ramanujan 'combined a power of generalisation, a feeling for form, and a capacity for rapid modification of his hypothesis, that were often really startling, and made him, in his own peculiar field, without a rival in his day'. During the five years Ramanujan was in England he had over twenty mathematical papers published, including several written in collaboration with Hardy.

In the spring of 1917 Ramanujan became seriously ill and spent some months being treated for pulmonary tuberculosis; it is now thought (see Young 1994) that he was probably suffering hepatic amoebiasis, a disease of the liver. Unfortunately the remote location of the sanatorium, which meant that he was cut off from his friends, combined with the Spartan regime and above all the lack of acceptable food, left him deeply depressed. One day in 1918 he attempted suicide. Even so, according to Neville, he never doubted his decision to come to England. Meanwhile Hardy, with Littlewood's support, did all he could to ensure that the genius of Ramanujan was recognised, including, in 1918, his election to the fellowship of the Royal Society, and to a Trinity fellowship. Soon afterwards, owing to concern over his state of health, arrangements were made for him to return to India, with the prospect of a professorship at the University of Madras. In 1919 he briefly took up the professorship; however, his health was by then quite poor. His mother and his wife continued their endless quarrels. He resisted medical treatment and died in Chetput, near Madras, on 26 April 1920 at the age of thirty-two. Until the end he remained passionately devoted to mathematics. His mother never recovered from his loss; her other sons had none of his genius. His wife, with no children of her own, was swindled out of her inheritance, and condemned to the wretched existence of so many widows in India until the occasion of his centennial drew attention to her plight. His mathematical reputation suffered something of an eclipse in the years immediately after his death, but more recently it has recovered and in his homeland he is now famous.

Neville, who knew Ramanujan well, summed up his character in these words: 'Perfect in manners, simple in manner, resigned in trouble and unspoilt by renown, grateful to a fault and devoted beyond measure to his friends, Ramanujan was a lovable man as well as a great mathematician' (Neville, cited in James 2002). Hardy said: 'I owe more to him than to anyone else in the world with one exception, and my association with him is the one romantic incident in my life' (Hardy, cited in James 2002). However, the source of Ramanujan's mathematical powers remains a mystery. It seems fairly clear that a phenomenal memory played some part in it, but precisely what books he had seen and what he had learned from them remains unknown; no one thought to ask him. Ramanujan himself attributed his exceptional powers to the family deity, the god Narasimha. A deeply religious man, he combined his passion with his faith, and once told a friend that 'an equation has no meaning for me unless it expresses a thought of God'. During dreams the most complicated mathematics used to unfold before him, he said. After waking he could set down on paper only a fraction of what was shown to him.

Acknowledgment

The biographical information in this chapter is based on James (2002). The other principal sources of information in this chapter are Fitzgerald (2004), Kanigel (1991) and Young (1994).

CHAPTER FOURTEEN

Ludwig Wittgenstein (*1889–1951*)

[Wittgenstein] was perhaps the most perfect example I have ever known of genius as traditionally conceived, passionate, profound, intense and dominating...his life was turbulent and troubled, and his personal force was extraordinary. (Bertrand Russell, cited in Monk 1990)

We have already encountered Ludwig Wittgenstein, one of the most original and influential philosophers of the twentieth century, in the profile of Bertrand Russell (Chapter 10). Several authorities have discussed the possibility that Wittgenstein's strange patterns of behaviour might be accounted for by Asperger's syndrome. Gillberg, for example, does so in *A Guide to Asperger Syndrome* (2002) and concludes that it is likely that he had an autism spectrum disorder that fitted almost to perfection the syndrome as outlined by Asperger. The Scottish psychiatrist Sula Wolff (1995) described his personality as schizoid but cautions that this should in no way be regarded as the most important aspect of his productive life, nor as the explanation of his genius. Fitzgerald provides a more extended psychobiography of his case in *Autism and Creativity* (2004) where he concludes that Wittgenstein was the perfect example of an autistic philosopher, whose autism had a direct impact on his thinking. It also placed limitations on his philosophy, which was excessively narrow and reductionist. Fitzgerald also draws attention to parallels between

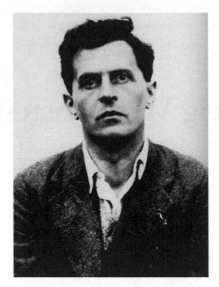

© The Master and Fellows of Trinity College Cambridge

Wittgenstein and Spinoza, who he believes may also have had Asperger's. Both philosophers tried to deal with bewildering social worlds by retreating into philosophy with an extraordinarily narrow focus. As Fitzgerald comments, more broadly based theories of philosophy require the philosopher to have a significant capacity for empathy that is much diminished in people with Asperger's.

Ludwig Wittgenstein was born in Vienna on 26 April 1889, the youngest of eight children. Three of his four brothers eventually committed suicide, as did one of his male cousins. An aunt of his suffered from a severe mental disorder, and he is said to have had a nephew with Asperger's syndrome. His paternal grandfather was described as having 'a stern, cold and forbidding expression and seriousness of conversation', and as being 'determined and not a little irascible'. Ludwig's father Carl Wittgenstein lacked empathy, and was harsh to his sons, from whom he demanded nothing less than perfection. Carl was dyslexic but possessed a phenomenal ability for mathematical calculations and was able to give a lecture with statistics, tables, etc. all without notes. Ludwig's mother Leopoldine (née Kalmus) was described as an anxious and insecure woman, unable to see her children as individuals in their own right. The family were dominated by her formidable husband, whom Ludwig worshipped.

Carl Wittgenstein was one of the wealthiest men in the Austro-Hungarian empire, with a fortune that was originally amassed in the steel industry and later on the stock market. Some called him the Austrian Carnegie. The Wittgensteins lived in patrician style; their opulent mansion was furnished with choice works of art, and the work of the secessionist painters was exhibited in it. Johannes Brahms was a frequent visitor; it seems likely that his clarinet quintet received its first performance in their house. Several members of the family were gifted musically, particularly Ludwig's brother Paul. In the First World War Paul lost his right arm on the eastern front; he successfully resumed his career as a concert pianist. Ravel wrote his well-known piano concerto for the left hand for him to perform.

The future philosopher did not speak well until after his fourth birthday; like his father he suffered from dyslexia throughout his life. In his youth he showed great interest in making models of various kinds, one of a sewing machine, for example. Until the age of fourteen his education was provided by governesses and private tutors; as a result he was ineligible for the Gymnasium. Instead Wittgenstein began his formal education at the Realschule in Linz, a school for scientific or technical education also attended by Adolf Schicklgruber, later known as Hitler. Wittgenstein's polite speech made him conspicuous at school, and inevitably he suffered from ridicule and bullying. He was short-sighted and below average in height. In schoolwork Wittgenstein did well in religion and in English, less so in mathematics and physics. Like other members of his family he was musically gifted. He had absolute pitch and at one time had ambitions to become an orchestral conductor. He also liked to whistle music and could do so with great accuracy and expression. Although three-quarters Jewish he was raised as a Catholic, with all his siblings, and took religion very seriously, but later lost his faith.

After leaving school, at the age of seventeen, Wittgenstein intended to study physics in Vienna under Ludwig Boltzmann. The great physicist's suicide in 1906 necessitated a major change of plan, and Wittgenstein went instead first to the famous Technische Hochschule in Berlin-Charlottenburg, where he studied engineering, and then for three years to the University of Manchester as a research student in the same field. His speciality was aeronautical engineering, then in its infancy; a new type of aircraft propeller he invented was patented. However, he also felt drawn towards mathematics, especially the foundations of the subject, and in 1912, after consulting the Austrian philosopher Frege, he went to Cambridge to study under Russell. He had done no systematic reading in the classics of philosophy but, as we know, Russell was impressed by the depth of Wittgenstein's thought and his intellectual passion.

At Cambridge Wittgenstein met an undergraduate named David Pinsent, one of the very few people who was ever really close to him, and with whom he fell in love, although Pinsent may have been quite unaware of this. He confided in Pinsent that ever since his schooldays he had suffered from a terrible feeling of loneliness and rejection; that he had continually thought of suicide and felt ashamed of never daring to kill himself. They went on a trip to Iceland together, during which Wittgenstein tried to teach Pinsent, a budding lawyer, about philosophy, especially symbolic logic. He told Pinsent he could not bear the company of other tourists. The next year they went to Norway together. Pinsent died in a flying accident at the end of the First World War. After hearing the news of this, Wittgenstein described him as his first and only friend.

Throughout his life, Wittgenstein appears only to have had occasional sexual relations with partners of either sex. Afterwards he would feel remorseful for not having returned the love and warmth extended to him by these partners. One woman became very affectionate towards him but he found this oppressive and in rejecting her wrote that 'her journalistic ways of expressing herself filled him with repugnance'. He could not see that his brutal openness and frankness could be seen as harsh and rejecting to the recipient of such a hurtful letter. Almost all his love objects were male and he could fall in love with people without their knowledge. Wittgenstein said of himself that he was unable to give affection. He could only handle relationships on his own terms and where he had total control.

Somewhat against Russell's wishes Wittgenstein was taken up by others in Russell's intellectual circle, including members of the Bloomsbury group. Maynard Keynes, for one, was fascinated by him. Wittgenstein was elected to the Apostles: the essay 'What is Philosophy?' that he presented as a new member lasted four minutes; shortly afterwards he resigned. One day early in 1913 Wittgenstein came to Russell in a state of great agitation saying that he had to leave Cambridge at once because his independent and eccentric elder sister Margarete had come to live in London with her American husband and he couldn't bear to be so near to them. Wittgenstein went off to spend the rest of the winter as a recluse in a log cabin on a Norwegian fjord north of Bergen, where he quickly learned Norwegian. When asked what else he had done there he said he spent the time praying.

As soon as the First World War began he returned to Vienna but then found he could not leave Austria again. He was very patriotic and, despite a hernia that had exempted him from the normal period of military service, he volunteered for the army and served for five years. He travelled in a naval vessel down the Vistula into Russian territory, and then to Krakow, before being sent to the front line. He got on badly with his comrades, whom he despised. After a period of active service he was posted to a reserve officer's training school in Moravia, where he found more congenial companions. In due course he was commissioned as an officer and returned to active service, this time on the Italian front. He appears to have been completely fearless, even during heavy fighting, and this earned him several medals; fearlessness is another Asperger characteristic. He was officially described as very intelligent, of serious character, outstandingly brave, most obedient, a good comrade. After the collapse of the Austro-Hungarian forces in 1918 he was taken prisoner by the Italians and held for almost a year. Most of the time he was in a prison camp near Monte Cassino, where he rejected efforts by influential friends to secure his release.

At intervals during the war Wittgenstein had been recording his ideas about philosophy in a series of notebooks that he carried around in his rucksack. These ideas resulted in the austere theory that he set out in his definitive *Tractatus Logico-philosophicus*, dedicated to Pinsent.

He sent it to Russell, who arranged for it to be published. Characteristically, Wittgenstein provided no explanations but simply made statements. Nevertheless, before long the treatise had changed the direction of twentieth-century linguistic philosophy. Later, he would gradually abandon what he had written in the *Tractatus* and replace it by another work, the *Philosophical Investigations*. He spent much of his later years constantly rearranging the material for this; it was not published until 1953, after his death.

After the death of his father in 1912 Wittgenstein had inherited a huge fortune. Almost at once he distributed some of this to various Austrian artists, and later he made a financial contribution to the Austrian war effort. After the end of the war he resolved to live as simply as possible, with the minimum of possessions, and gave away almost everything he possessed not for charitable purposes, but to his brother and sisters. He explained that the poor might be corrupted by his generosity but not the relatively rich. We may recall that at his death Cavendish returned his fortune to the wealthy family from which it came (Chapter 6).

Meanwhile Wittgenstein, feeling that he had said all he wanted to about philosophy, had decided to become a schoolteacher. After some teacher training, during which he learnt to play the clarinet, he taught primary schoolchildren in a remote part of Austria for six years. He was in constant friction with the local people, who he treated with contempt; parents and children alike appear to have considered him a major problem. The children he taught came from poor families, but nevertheless he made unrealistic plans for the most talented to go on to higher education, without consulting their parents who would not be able to afford to pay for this. In class he was very frightening to his pupils and would sometimes hit them very hard if they did not live up to his expectations. He boxed their ears and pulled their hair. After he was prosecuted for the physical abuse of one boy he gave up schoolteaching.

Next Wittgenstein worked briefly as assistant gardener at the Benedictine monastery of Klosterneuburg, near Vienna, and for a while thought of becoming a monk. Then a more attractive opportunity arose. His sister Margarete had appointed an architect to design a house for her in Vienna. She found Wittgenstein taking a great interest in the project and eventually had to let him take over. Although not qualified as an architect, he had some competence in that profession, and the resultant building, rather bleak-looking and with few concessions to domestic comfort, is his work down to the smallest detail. The horizontal lines and the materials – concrete, glass and steel – reflect Wittgenstein's training in engineering and preference for minimalism. Later he remarked to a colleague that philosophy was hard enough, but 'it is nothing compared to the difficulties involved in architecture.'

In 1929 Wittgenstein returned to Cambridge, where he was awarded a PhD and a five-year fellowship at Trinity. 'The university atmosphere nauseates me,' he complained, 'the stiffness, the artificiality, the self-satisfaction of the people.' A brilliant mathematics student, Francis Skinner, half his age, now fell in love with him and they had a sexual relationship. This troubled Wittgenstein, who at the time thought that sex was incompatible with love. Wittgenstein persuaded this gifted young man, who had become crippled at the age of thirteen, to give up mathematics and become an apprentice mechanic in a firm making scientific instruments; he had given similarly unwelcome career advice to other promising students, much to their dismay. Skinner remained close to Wittgenstein until his untimely death from polio in 1941.

Wittgenstein was well read in the English and German classics, but among novelists his favourite authors were the Russians Dostoevsky and Tolstoy. In 1934 he decided to learn Russian, partly so as to read their works in the original and partly because he was planning to visit the Soviet Union. His Russian teacher, who got to know him well, described him as having the keen look of a bird in flight, as being stern and forbidding yet naive, unaware that he cast a spell and held others in thrall with his talk, elusive, and surrounding his comings and goings with mystery. She wrote: 'I could never look on his ability to find out the weak spots of another human being and hit out hard as anything but a flaw. The knowledge that he was at the same time a man of great purity and innocence cannot alter my feeling.' Many examples are on record of his personal hypersensitivity but insensitivity to the feelings of others. He had an endless capacity for finding fault with other people and was extremely observant of their shortcomings. He considered he needed 'robustness and understanding' from others when some trivial inconvenience or misunderstanding caused an emotional outburst.

In 1939 Wittgenstein was elected professor of philosophy at Cambridge and fellow of Trinity. Although most of his colleagues respected his genius and tolerated his eccentricity, they regarded him as withdrawn, mysterious, inaccessible, eccentric, even somewhat mad. He dressed carefully but oddly for his day, always wearing the same type of clothes: light grey flannel trousers, flannel open-necked shirt, and leather or woollen jacket. A former pupil described his remarkable facial appearance: 'He was very withdrawn, had a huge great forehead, very penetrating eyes, but above all, when he concentrated, standing up talking to someone, so many anxiety lines appeared on his forehead that they made a chequer board.' Norman Malcolm, one of Wittgenstein's most successful students, recalled that during his classes the professor would be wrestling with his thoughts, often falling into silences that no one dared to interrupt. When a topic under discussion caught his attention he would become utterly engrossed, oblivious of his surroundings. When he entertained students there was never any small talk, just long periods of silence. While his guests sat in deckchairs he would offer them refreshments from chemical beakers, saying he found ordinary chinaware too ugly.

Wittgenstein was still oppressed by feelings of guilt and shame. Memories of his disastrous time as a schoolteacher haunted him. When he returned to the place where he taught in order to apologise for his conduct, he only succeeded in further upsetting the families of his former pupils. He brooded on this in a paper that he called a 'confession', which also dealt with other unhappy episodes in his life, such as his unsatisfactory sexual experiences; on one occasion he read this aloud in a restaurant, much to the embarrassment of those around him – he lacked any sense of propriety. In the paper he also dwelt on the fact that he was three-quarters Jewish. Strangely, in spite of his high intelligence and rigid moral principles, Wittgenstein seems not to have been particularly worried by the possible consequences of Hitler's rise to power in Germany.

Wittgenstein was celebrated for the gaiety of his conversation – he was an excellent mimic. Yet according to the writer Iris Murdoch, he was feared in Cambridge because of his shocking frankness and lack of any social graces. She found him extremely frightening and felt terrified by just being near him. Whatever other people might say to him, even when it was a matter of their personal opinions or feelings, he would interrupt them to say something like 'No, that's not the point' or just 'You are wrong.' According to Malcolm (1984), he 'always spoke emphatically and with a distinctive intonation…his voice was resonant, the pitch being somewhat higher than that of the normal male voice. His words came out, not fluently but with great force.'

Wittgenstein was quoted as saying 'normal human beings are a balm to me but a torment at the same time'. From his schooldays onwards, he could not get on with most of the people around him. While in the army, during the First World War, he found the baseness of his comrades frightful and volunteered for night duty to escape their company. Yet later, as a rural elementary schoolteacher, he sought out the company of manual workers. During the Second World War he worked as a medical orderly in a London hospital, delivering medication to the wards; when he did so he advised patients not to take what he had brought them. Later he was more usefully employed as a trauma researcher in a clinical laboratory in Newcastle, where no one was supposed to know he was a university professor. His work on the physiology of shock impressed the head of the laboratory.

Soon after the end of the war Wittgenstein resigned from his Cambridge chair, and went off to live an isolated life in Ireland, first on a remote farm, and then in a hut on the west coast. His immediate neighbours shunned him, because they thought he was mad, and they forbade him to walk on their land, because they thought he would frighten their sheep. Malcolm, who had become professor of philosophy at Cornell University in the United States, invited Wittgenstein to visit him in Ithaca. When his wife offered him rye bread and cheese for his first lunch, he liked this so much that he would eat nothing else during his stay. On one occasion Malcolm took his visitor along to a seminar. Someone in the audience remarked that Wittgenstein looked like a tramp, taken into the warmth on account of Malcolm's generous nature. Malcolm described Wittgenstein at this time as suspicious of other people's motives and both precipitous and often erroneous in his judgements.

By 1950 Wittgenstein's health was giving cause for concern. His doctor, Edward Bevan, diagnosed cancer of the prostate, and told him he had not long to live. His first action was to make a last visit to the family home in Vienna. A few months later he returned to England, and by the New Year he was back in Cambridge. By this time he needed constant medical attention. In February 1951 the kindly Bevans took him into their home, since he had a horror of ending his life in hospital, and he died there on 29 April 1951. Although morbid fears haunted his early years, his later years seem to have been brighter. His last words, when told friends were coming to see him the next day, are reported to have been: 'Tell them I've had a wonderful life.'

Acknowledgment

The principal sources of information in this chapter are Berman, Fitzgerald and Hayes (1996), Engelmann (1967), Fitzgerald (2004), Malcolm (1984), McGuiness (1988), Monk (1990) and Wright (1990).

CHAPTER FIFTEEN

Alfred Kinsey
(1894–1956)

Kinsey as a biologist could not transcend narrow materialist thinking; he has an awkwardness in the handling of ideas. (Lionel Trilling 1948)

After Thomas Jefferson it is not hard to find other Asperger possibles from the United States, for example the Civil War general Stonewall Jackson (Fitzgerald 2002). However, the next American to be profiled here is the biologist Alfred Kinsey. When the first Kinsey report was published the author found himself hailed as a sexual liberator, his name a household word. Fifty years after his death the institute for sex research he founded continues to flourish. Fitzgerald (1999b) has argued that Kinsey meets the criteria for Asperger's syndrome.

Alfred Charles Kinsey was born on 23 June 1894 in the teeming industrial city of Hoboken, on the Hudson River opposite Manhattan. His harsh and puritanical father Alfred Seguine Kinsey had worked his way up to become instructor in mechanical engineering at the Stevens Institute of Technology, in Hoboken. His mother Sarah Ann (née Charles) was the daughter of a carpenter; she was as deeply religious as her husband but poorly educated. Alfred was their first child; later a daughter Mildred Elisabeth and another son Robert Benjamin completed the family.

Kinsey had an unhappy childhood. He suffered from rickets, which left him hump-shouldered for life, and rheumatic fever, which doctors feared had damaged his heart. He also caught typhoid. As a result of these illnesses he often missed school and was unable to take part in the normal rough and tumble of boyhood. His mother was over-protective, while his father, a hard man, was slow to praise, quick to find fault. Life began to improve for Alfred when he was ten years old and the family moved away from unhealthy Hoboken to the suburb of South Orange, set in pleasant countryside west of Newark.

Kinsey was always reading or practising the piano. He had hopes of becoming a professional pianist, but he was not good enough. There was little social life at home and he made no friends. At the local high school, his main academic interest was botany. He took up some hobbies, first collecting gramophone records, then postage stamps. Bird watching was his next enthusiasm. He also joined the Boy Scouts, and took up hiking with such determination that his parents sent him to see a cardiologist who decided that, after all, his heart had not been damaged by rheumatic fever.

Outwardly Kinsey appeared to be a fairly normal American boy but inwardly he was profoundly troubled. 'He was more or less a loner,' said one of his classmates. 'Everybody liked him, you know, but he just wasn't one of the guys. He never did fit in right, was unsure of himself socially, ill-at-ease with others.' He had an obsession with personal cleanliness. Adolescence was the time when he became skilled at concealing his inner life. He had no social contact with girls and began to suspect that he had homosexual inclinations. Later the man who had been sickly in youth and the only boy in his class not to play in a body-contact sport became 'a big husky fellow, a rugged, hardy man looking much younger than his age'.

When Kinsey graduated from high school he wanted to go to college and study biology. However, his father was determined that his son should go to the Stevens Institute where he taught, and be trained as an engineer. The reluctant Kinsey just scraped through the entrance examination for Stevens, but after two years he decided to leave. This led to a major confrontation with his father who refused to provide him with any further financial support.

Kinsey enrolled at Bowdoin, the small liberal arts college in New Brunswick, Maine, that had a good reputation for biology. He soon earned a reputation as a deadly serious student; he was determined to succeed. Although he joined a fraternity, he took little interest in its social activities. He was ill at ease in the company of others, quite unable to make small talk. At the piano his style of playing was described as tempestuous; his repertoire was limited to classical music, not popular music and certainly not ragtime. He shone in the debating society. The First World War was approaching and there were important issues to be debated, often in contests between rival college teams. When he graduated *summa cum laude* he was chosen as valetudinarian and elected class president.

Kinsey left Bowdoin with a scholarship for Harvard and began post-graduate work in biology at the celebrated Bussey Institute, where he was determined to make a name for himself. He specialised in the study of gall wasps, from which he expected to learn something new about evolution. When he submitted his doctorate thesis on these tiny insects he was awarded a travelling scholarship that he used to make an extended tour of the south-western United States, collecting the eggs of different species. Several institutions were interested in recruiting this promising young biologist, but in the end he accepted an assistant professorship at Indiana University. This was not an elite school like Harvard but admitted students with a wide range of abilities.

At the university Kinsey soon made himself unpopular. He was disrespectful of his seniors, prickly, domineering and stubborn. In conversation he could abruptly turn hostile. Everyone recognised his ability, but avoided him, because there was something in his personality that made him want to control other people. Despite his youth Kinsey was highly opinionated and domineering, pressing his views on anyone who disagreed with him. One of his former students recalled:

> He was a commanding presence. Both in appearance and in demeanour he was all business, in dress he was conservative. He was a tall man, who wore his fair hair in a crew-cut, his shoulders

somewhat stooped. Peering out from behind horn-rimmed
spectacles were large eyes with lids that drooped right over
them. He entered the classroom on the dot, walking in long
measured rather brisk steps without a glance at his audience. His
voice was strongly modulated, his enunciation precise. His
lectures were a model of clarity and precision, but addressed to
gifted students rather than the mediocre. (Fitzgerald 1999b)

At Bloomington Kinsey made an effort to build up a social life for
himself through nature hikes and camping, but the relationships he
formed in this way were casual and superficial. The friends of his
maturity were all work-centred. He remained emotionally isolated
until he met Clara Bracken McMillen, a brilliant undergraduate
student majoring in chemistry. Friendly, competent, self-possessed and
secure, she was unafraid to make the first move. They were married in
1921 and went off on an extended honeymoon, consisting of a
camping expedition in the White Mountains of New Hampshire. They
had three children. A son born in 1922 died at an early age. A daughter
Ann was born two years later, and finally another son Bruce in 1928.
Kinsey adored Bruce when he was young; his personality traits resembled his father's. Kinsey was very fond of children.

Music remained important to Kinsey. When electrical recording
came in he built up a huge collection of gramophone records that he
would play to an invited audience. Those present on these occasions
were expected to sit quite still and not make a sound while the music
was being played. One of them found the experience 'much too
formal, much too frozen, much too strict for my liking, deeply unset-
tling – somewhat horrific'. Kinsey would search the faces of the guests,
hoping to share the emotional response they could feel but he could
not. He was also a fanatically keen gardener, specialising in irises.
Because Kinsey seldom spoke about his childhood many had the
impression that he came from a well-to-do family as his eastern accent,
his educational pedigree (Bowdoin undergraduate, Harvard graduate
school) and his knowledge of classical music rather suggested. They
found Kinsey cool and aloof, every inch a portrait of old money. They
were unaware of his true background in the slums of Hoboken.

Kinsey loved entomological field trips, amassing vast quantities of gall wasps, far beyond any reasonable scientific purpose. He enjoyed summer camps and on one of them he fell head over heels in love with a young man, the first of several such affairs in the years to come. This seemed to liberate him from some of his sexual inhibitions; he became increasingly preoccupied with sex, as we shall see. Unusually for that period he believed the sex education of children, then dealt with at school if at all, should be undertaken by parents at an early stage. At home during the summer, the Kinseys went around almost nude. Meanwhile the entomological research that he regarded as so important was meeting with criticism. He wrote several biological textbooks, mainly to supplement his income but also to promote his ideas on evolutionary biology.

When the long-serving president of Indiana University retired he was succeeded by a much younger man, who replaced many of the older and weaker faculty members by new blood. Among other reforms he set out to introduce sex education at the university, and Kinsey volunteered to take charge of this. He began by teaching a non-credit marriage course for seniors, in which he took a matter-of-fact biological approach, intended to liberate the young men and women from sexual repression. As part of the course they were asked to complete detailed questionnaires, the precursors of Kinsey's case histories. Finding these questionnaires inappropriate and open to errors in interpretation, he began conducting face-to-face interviews, initially held in a corner of his busy laboratory. Soon he was actively engaged in counselling individual students about their sex lives. Kinsey impressed students on the marriage courses as earnest and sympathetic, in contrast to the arrogant and gruff image he had routinely projected in biology classes. By 1940 the marriage course had been opened to all students, not only seniors, and it grew so popular that enrolment soon reached 400 students per semester. Other universities began to put on similar courses. While sex education was important to Kinsey, he was increasingly using it as a springboard for the research that was to take over his life. The data he was collecting from students was just a beginning.

Kinsey's growing involvement in sex research did not go unnoticed. The president came under strong pressure from the trustees of the university, who wanted Kinsey brought to heel. He told Kinsey that he must choose between giving the marriage course, with modifications, and pursuing his research activities. Kinsey resisted strongly, with support from the students if not from his colleagues, but in the end he had to give way, and decided to give up the course and concentrate on the research. He realised that in order to obtain meaningful results he needed a more general human sample than the university could provide. He began to travel out of town to conduct interviews with additional subjects. At first these trips were only at weekends, but as his interest grew his time away from the campus increased and he began to venture further afield. He took a particular interest in the gay communities of Chicago and other mid-western cities.

During the 1940s, Kinsey embarked on the large-scale study of the sexual habits of men and women that was to dominate the rest of his life. He increased the number of out-of-town interviews and spent long hours interpreting data and training interviewers. Initially his resources were limited, and he used his own money to hire staff and pay expenses, but before long he received his first outside grant, which helped to reassure the university that he was doing something worthwhile. When a high-powered committee visited Bloomington to report on his activities he impressed them by showing that he could extract the information he needed not only from students but just as well from prisoners at the local jail. However, they were worried that Kinsey's peculiar personality would be a problem. Never before had they encountered anyone so frightfully focused, so suspicious and contemptuous of the work of others, and so unnervingly sure of himself. One of them described Kinsey as 'the most intense person I ever knew outside of an institute for psychiatry'. In 1943 Kinsey received a $23,000 grant from the National Research Council; over the next decade he received hundreds of thousands of dollars from the same source. The funding enabled him to establish an Institute for Sex Research at Indiana University as the base for his operations; after a good deal of argument this was set up as a private corporation, supported by the university but not part of it. Since the National Research Council was partly funded by the better-known Rockefeller Foundation, Kinsey began to describe the institute as supported by the foundation, and to by-pass the National Research Council. This was to have unfortunate repercussions later on.

The funding enabled Kinsey to hire more assistants; he took great care over their selection and trained them up to be loyal disciples. Soon the quantity of data collected, from some 18,000 face-to-face interviews, was enough to provide the material for a number of publications. A series of nine reports was planned, but Kinsey would live long enough to complete only two. The first one, on the human male, took him two years to write and rewrite. It included frank descriptions of biological functions and was entirely non-judgemental. Kinsey reported his findings simply and directly, correcting various false assumptions. In particular he reported that extramarital and premarital sex were more common than generally believed, that nearly all males, especially teenagers, masturbate, that masturbation did not cause mental illness, and that one in three males experienced at least one homosexual encounter in their lifetimes. In an attempt to stress the scientific nature of the work rather than its potentially more sensational aspects, he decided to give the report to a well-established medical firm, although more commercial publishers were in hot pursuit.

To avoid possible trouble for the university, the Kinsey Report was published while the State legislature was in recess. Entitled *The Sexual Behavior of the Human Male,* it sold 185,000 copies in its first year in print and made the *New York Times* best-seller list. Early polls indicated that most American readers agreed with his findings. The most vehement criticism came, as expected, from conservative and religious organisations. Most of these attacks were emotionally rather than scientifically based, but some were undeniably cogent. He was very upset by unfavourable reviews; few of his colleagues came to his defence. Moreover the growing criticism jeopardised Kinsey's relationship with the officers of the Rockefeller Foundation. Kinsey's mission, they came to realise, was to use science to attack traditional morality and promote an ethic of tolerance. Science was not merely his profession, it had become his religion.

When the first report appeared, the press described him as a man who used his charming personality to excellent advantage in getting men, women and children from all social levels to confide in him secrets that most of them certainly had never told anyone else. Journalists wrote of his easy-going, tolerant, easy-to-talk-with personality that permitted him to gain quick contact with people and speedy confidence of all kinds and conditions of men and women. One wrote:

> I'm as inhibited as the next fellow in sexual matters, but to my great surprise I experienced no embarrassment in giving intimate details of my personal life to this amazingly skilful interviewer. Kinsey played the role of a father-figure. Conversationally he is brisk, direct, sure of himself. He smiles readily and has a nice turn of humour, which saves his self-assurance from bordering on the obnoxious.

By 1949 the battle with his critics was taking a heavy toll. His response to pressure was to spend more and more time at work. Friends pleaded with him to take a vacation or at least catch up on his sleep. He lived in fear that his health would fail and he would die before his life's work was completed. In public Kinsey found himself increasingly on the defensive. In scholarly reviews of the first report by Lionel Trilling (1948) and others, the statistical and methodological aspects of his work were criticised. One problem was that his sample consisted only of volunteers and was not a true cross-section of the population at large; another that, although the report purported to be objective, it was in fact quite subjective. After a heated debate the Rockefeller board agreed to continue to support Kinsey, but he was warned this might be the last time. Meanwhile there were other problems. The institute housed Kinsey's personal collection of erotica (when members of the university art department came to view it he treated them to an interminable lecture; they became 'very, very bored'). By federal law US Customs were required to seize any erotica being imported; and this included some material ordered for the collection.

Kinsey decided to take the Customs to court when negotiations broke down, and he pursued the hopeless case with characteristic intensity.

According to close friends, Kinsey did not particularly like women or feel comfortable in their presence. There were no major differences in the way women were interviewed but he believed they were not as sexually responsive as men and made little effort to conceal this. He started writing the second Kinsey report, on the human female, in the summer of 1951 and continued, with numerous interruptions, for the next eighteen months. Ever the perfectionist he devoted even more care to it than he had done to the first report. If he had simply published his data and left it at that there would have been no trouble, but he went on to give his opinions on all kinds of related matters. *The Sexual Behavior of the Human Female* is an astonishingly provocative and highly personal work. It reveals in stark relief the scientific philosophy and methodology, the private passions, values and prejudices, the social agenda and above all the inner conflicts of the author.

The second report, as Kinsey expected, also soared up the best-seller charts, eventually reaching sales of a quarter million in the United States alone. There was enormous publicity, and less adverse criticism than there had been of the first. Some of the book's more controversial findings concerned the low rate of frigidity, high rates of premarital and extramarital sex, the rapidity of erotic response, and a detailed discussion of clitoral versus vaginal orgasm. Nevertheless there was harsh criticism, particularly from the religious right. Kinsey's methods and motives were again questioned. This was the period of McCarthyite witch-hunts. The tax-exempt foundations were under suspicion of helping to finance communism and socialism in America, and the Rockefeller Foundation was one of those liable to be investigated by a congressional committee. The non-political Kinsey found himself branded as a subversive and accused of furthering the communist cause by undermining American morals. Evangelist Billy Graham pronounced that 'it is impossible to estimate the damage this book will do to the already deteriorating morals of America'. The foundation's continuing support for Kinsey's institute made it seem vulnerable to such attacks. At the university the president and faculty stoutly defended Kinsey, but the foundation succumbed to political pressure and the axe fell. The National Research Council followed suit.

Meanwhile Kinsey's private behaviour was becoming increasingly strange. In the attic of his house he practised all kinds of sexual escapades, and arranged for them to be filmed. Members of the institute staff were coerced into taking part. He went to Peru with his colleagues to photograph a private collection of erotic ceramics. Soon after arriving there he was taken ill, and when he returned to Bloomington a period of convalescence was necessary before he could plunge himself back into work. Before long he was taken ill again and the pattern repeated itself. He had trouble sleeping, and became trapped in a cycle of tranquillisers and stimulants. When his heart started to give trouble he was hospitalised several times. Friends thought his heart attacks were brought on by his anger and frustration at the way he had been treated. Meanwhile the institute struggled on, supported mainly by royalties from the Kinsey reports. He played the role of guru, surrounded by disciples. Another report was planned, this time on sex offenders, so the institute turned its attention to interviewing prisoners who had been convicted of sex offences. Kinsey seemed to identify with the sex offenders he interviewed.

In 1955 friends concerned about his health persuaded him to travel to Europe for the first time. In London he was horrified by the behaviour of the prostitutes and their clientele. Such rampant prostitution, he thought, could only be due to sexual repression; he concluded that a lot of the American attitudes he deplored must have come from Britain. On the Continent he saw that other nations had succeeded in managing human sexuality with less repression, guilt and pain than the United States: 'I never realised that I could learn so much more about sex as I did in the seven weeks in Europe.' After returning to Bloomington he went back to work again, against medical advice. 'If I can't work,' he said, 'I would rather die.' The end came on 25 August 1956 when Kinsey died of pneumonia and heart complications at the age of 62. His two major works broke new ground in the field of sex research and led to more open and honest investigations of sexual practices.

Asperger's syndrome would account for many aspects of Kinsey's idiosyncracies. For example, he had an obsession with cleanliness. He was maladroit. He had a peculiar sense of humour, dry, teasing and sardonic, with the very loud laugh that is typical of the humourless. He had no small talk and was uneasy in social situations. There is much else, above all the exceptional energy and determination he displayed in pursuit of his objectives, first gall wasps and then sex research. Altogether the evidence supports Fitzgerald's (1999b) opinion that Kinsey is another Asperger possible.

Acknowledgment

The principal sources of information in this chapter are Fitzgerald (1999b), Gaythorne-Hardy (1998) and Jones (1997).

CHAPTER SIXTEEN

Simone Weil (1909–1943)

> She looked as if she belonged to another order of being; her mind didn't seem to belong to our age or our milieu. She felt like a very old soul. (A former schoolmate, cited in du Plessix Gray 2001)

We now return to France for the profile of someone whose life story haunts the imagination. She was a fortunate child, destined to grow up into a beautiful and intelligent young woman. However, among the good fairies who brought blessings to her cradle was a wicked witch, who was intent on doing her harm. The witch brought her migraine, which plagued her all her life, and anorexia, which undermined her health. She brought her a profound feeling of worthlessness and a strong tendency for self-mortification. And perhaps she also brought her Asperger's syndrome, which is at best a mixed blessing. In most respects Simone was not a particularly original thinker but she expressed herself well. Her political writings are now mainly of historical interest. On religion what she wrote had a mystic quality; for example, 'On reaching a certain degree of pain we lose the world but afterwards comes peace when we find it again.' Although she displayed an almost superhuman humility and what appears to be an almost outrageous arrogance, wrote the poet T.S. Eliot (Preface to Weil 1952), Simone Weil possessed a kind of genius akin to that of the saints.

Simone Weil was born in Paris on 3 February 1909. Her father Bernhard, born in Alsace, was a physician, utterly absorbed in the practice of his profession; her Russian-born mother Salomea (née Reinherz) was of a wealthy Viennese family. Both parents were non-orthodox Jewish, completely devoted to traditional conceptions of high French culture. Simone, born a month prematurely, was a sickly child. As an infant she did not thrive; in adolescence she sometimes thought she might have been poisoned by her mother's milk. An appendectomy at the age of three so traumatised her that whenever a stranger came to visit she would leave for fear he might be a doctor. Her mother pampered and cosseted her hypersensitive and moody daughter: 'She is indomitable, impossible to control, with an indescribable stubbornness that neither her father nor I can make a dent in,' she told a friend when Simone was five. Her elder brother André, three years her senior, was already showing unusual ability. By nine he was solving quite difficult mathematical problems, by twelve he had taught himself classical Greek and Sanskrit, and could play the violin. André had taught his sister to read as a birthday present for his father; she would master Greek and several modern languages in her early teens. The siblings often communicated with each other in spontaneously rhymed couplets, or in ancient Greek. When reciting scenes from Corneille or Racine they corrected each other with a slap in the face when one of them made a mistake or missed a beat. Theirs was a hermetic rarified world, barely accessible to outsiders.

Mme Weil, the dominant parent, was as scrupulous about her children's physical well-being as she was about their education. A phobic dread of microbes ruled her household. She insisted that her children should not be kissed by anyone outside the immediate family. By the time she was four Simone refused even to be kissed by her parents, and for the rest of her life she displayed a revulsion for most forms of physical contact. Although the children never rebelled overtly against their coddling parents, they became very good at manipulating them. One game was to go knocking on the doors of neighbours to beg for food, pleading that their parents were letting them starve. Another was to go out bare-legged in the depths of winter, pretending to passers-by that their parents neglected to provide them with stockings. At table the cosmopolitan Weils often talked in German or English rather than French. Although Mme Weil kept a kosher kitchen, it was not until after the First World War that the children learnt that they were Jewish.

By the age of ten Simone began to display strong sensitivity to issues of social justice. She was appalled by the manner in which the Treaty of Versailles humiliated the defeated enemy. She followed the course of the Russian Revolution quite closely in the newspapers and told classmates she was a Bolshevik. Simone found it hard to accept that her brother was not just a mathematical prodigy; he had a genius for the subject. At the age of twelve he was solving mathematical problems beyond the doctoral level; he also was reading Plato and Homer in the original Greek. At the age of fourteen, three years before the normal minimum age, he took the baccalauréat with the highest scores in the country, and started preparing for the fiercely competitive entrance examinations for the Ecole Normale Supérieure. At the age of fifteen he took these and again came out top of the list for the whole country. Much later she recorded her thoughts in her spiritual autobiography:

> At fourteen I fell into one of those fits of bottomless despair which come with adolescence, and I seriously thought of dying because of the mediocrity of my natural faculties. The exceptional gifts of my brother, who had a childhood and youth comparable to those of Pascal, brought my own inferiority home to me...after months of inward darkness, I suddenly had the everlasting conviction that no matter what human being, even though practically devoid of natural faculties, can penetrate to the kingdom of truth reserved for genius, if only he longs for truth and perpetually concentrates all his attention upon its attainment. (du Plessix Gray 2001)

Simone was starting to develop one of her main characteristics, not shared with André, namely an almost pathological receptiveness to the sufferings of others and a strong tendency to cultivate her own. Although Simone put enormous energy into her schoolwork and excelled in most subjects, she failed in cartography and drawing because of a specific handicap: her hands, disproportionately small for her fairly large-boned body, were unusually weak and maladroit. Also she wrote sloppily and slowly, another sign of motor clumsiness. Periods at prestigious girls' schools alternated with periods of private tuition. The Lycée Henri IV prepared students for entry into the Grandes Ecoles. In the years she spent there she came under the influence of the renowned teacher and writer Emile-Auguste Chartier, better known as Alain.

Simone was already suffering from acute headaches and from feelings of extreme worthlessness. She now started to suffer from anorexia nervosa, and became terribly undernourished. She was a typical anorexic, just as Mme Weil was a fine example of an anorexic's mother. Simone decided to create a new persona for herself that would not change much for the rest of her life. A mass of uncombed black hair and huge tortoiseshell-framed glasses nearly obscured her small delicate face. Those who met her for the first time were struck by the large, bold, inquisitive dark eyes that scrutinised others with an almost indiscreet curiosity. Her features were lovely but brusque and awkward, and she was pitifully thin. An even more forbidding aspect of her appearance was the drab unisex clothing with which she covered her angular body. Her garments were always the same – a cape, boyish flat-heeled shoes, a long full skirt and a long body-obscuring jacket in dark colours. Apart from an occasional wool beret, she never wore a hat, which in that decade was most unusual for a young woman of her class. Her dress was matched by her increasingly radical politics. Although terrified of any sexual encounter, she mixed happily with men throughout her life. The beauty of her porcelain skin, of her delicate features, continued to be all but hidden by her huge glasses, her grubby clothes and her awkward gait. She remained as averse to physical contact as she had been in childhood, shunning even the most casual of hugs or comradely linking of elbows.

As for her manner, she retained the argumentative eccentric style she had developed in her mid-teens, which had become ever more intransigent. Eager to enjoy intense friendships, she chose her friends imperiously; but when she discovered an unfavourable trait in one of them, she was capable of abruptly ending the relationship with a horizontal cutting gesture of her hand. 'There was rudeness and rawness of her manners, her unusual appearance and above all, the battering of those ruthless judgements,' said a close friend. 'I can still see her,' said another, 'crouched over her notebook, her fingers often covered with ink-stains, writing very slowly and painfully, quick to turn her head, attentive to everything, observing things ardently from behind her thick glasses.' On the street she put herself and anyone with her at constant risk, talking and gesticulating as she walked through traffic with long jerky steps, totally heedless of cars and escaping them by sheer chance. In spite of her extreme ineptitude for sport she joined the first women's rugby football team in France, formed at the Femina athletic club in Paris. She invariably returned from the playing field covered with mud and bruises.

Simone's insistence on practising the politics she preached was equally awesome. She was a strong supporter of trade unions, and would later become an activist. At this stage she made a start by helping to found an association called the Social Education Group that offered evening classes in mathematics, physics, sociology and political economy to railway workers. In the spring of 1923 she was accepted for the Ecole Normale Supérieure, just like her brother, with the highest national ranking of that year's applicants. It was only the second year that women had been eligible, and when she arrived she found she was the sole woman in her year.

Normaliens may attend lectures at the Sorbonne or not, as they please; Simone did not. In fact she had little to do with the faculty at the Normale either, but continued to attend Alain's classes at the nearby lycée. She graduated successfully at the end of the course and began the ten years of lycée teaching required of normaliens. Meanwhile she took a variety of temporary jobs involving manual labour, in farming and fishing, for example, before starting teaching in Le Puy, the first post to which she had been assigned. Her possessive mother came along to help her settle in, and stayed with her as she was moved around in the course of her teaching assignments. Simone taught philosophy at Le Puy and also gave courses in Greek and art history, constantly rumpling her hair as she delivered her lectures in a monotonous tone of voice, without lifting her eyes from the text. Although most of the students failed her courses, they were amused by her awkwardness, her clumsy way of holding chalk, for example. With her threadbare vestments and her naked sandalled feet, she reminded them of some medieval hermit. The halo of voluntary poverty, the ascetic disarray of her life, touched them deeply.

> The clumsiness of her gestures, above all of her hands, her piercing look through her thick glasses, her smile – everything about her emanating feelings of total frankness and forgetfulness of self, revealing a nobility of soul that was certainly at the root of the emotions she inspired in us. (du Plessix Gray 2001)

By 1932 Hitler's rise to power was under way and Simone wanted to find out for herself just why so many German workers supported the Nazi movement. She went to live with a communist family in Berlin and returned to France deeply pessimistic about the future. When she wrote newspaper articles about the situation, she made no mention of the rabid anti-Semitism. Her long-suffering parents were expected to put up with a steady stream of Simone's radical friends, on one occasion Leon Trotsky and his wife, who arrived with two armed bodyguards. She was no longer a supporter of the Bolsheviks, quite the reverse; she developed an undying hatred for the Soviet regime, 'a bureaucratic, military and police dictatorship that has nothing socialist or communist about it but the name'.

Although Simone wanted nothing to do with sexuality herself, she was intrigued by other people's sex lives. She was fascinated by prostitutes, for example, and visited one brothel disguised as a man; when she was found out she was nearly lynched. She wrote a lengthy article, *Oppression and Liberty*, essentially her political testament. She decided to take a year off teaching in order to have some experience of unskilled factory work. Her first job was with the Alstom firm, manufacturers of large-scale electrical machinery, where she was given an exceptionally arduous job, feeding copper bars into a furnace. She was humiliated and bullied by the foremen. After seven weeks she fell ill and left the factory, which she described as like a penal institution. Her next job was at a smaller firm, equally unpleasant; this lasted a month. Finally she got a job at the Renault plant, where she survived the trial period and was kept on for some months working on the production line. To avoid feeling guilty about taking such jobs at a time of high unemployment she contributed her wages towards relief for the unemployed.

In September 1935, after leaving Renault, she took a holiday in Portugal with her parents. There she saw something that transformed her life:

> In a wretched state physically, I entered the little Portuguese village that was, alas, very wretched too, on the very day of the festival of its patron saint. I was alone. It was evening and there was a full moon over the sea. The fishermen's wives were making a tour of all the ships in procession. Carrying candles and singing very ancient hymns of a heart-rending sadness. There the conviction suddenly came to me that Christianity is the religion of slaves, that slaves cannot help belonging to it, I amongst others. (du Plessix Gray 2001)

The next year, when civil war broke out in Spain, thousands of people from other countries came to help the Republicans fight the Fascists, who were being sent supplies from Germany and manpower from Italy. While Simone approved the French government's decision not to become involved, she went to Spain to join the nucleus of what would become the International Brigade, in the role of reporter for a trade union magazine. Later she joined the militia and learned how to handle a rifle, albeit with her usual clumsiness. One night, near-sighted as she was awkward, she put her foot in a pot of boiling cooking oil and was badly burnt. Her parents, who had been desperately looking for her, came to the rescue and took her back to France. Soon afterwards the unit she had joined was wiped out by the opposing troops. She made a first visit to Italy and in Assisi took another step on the road towards the Christian faith. She rejected Judaism, especially the Old Testament of the Bible, but then decided that this also prevented her from joining a Christian church. At the same time she became increasingly disillusioned with the various left-wing movements she had previously supported.

Throughout this time Simone had been plagued by migraine and the time arrived when she had to give up teaching altogether. She spent Holy Week of 1938 at Solesmes, a Benedictine abbey in north-east France, another powerful mystical experience. In politics she was now strongly pacifist, oblivious of the threat the Nazis posed to the Jews. When the war came, and the fall of France, she and her parents escaped to the south, where the puppet government in Vichy was nominally in control. The aim was to get to America, although Simone intended to go on from there to England and join the Free French. Many others were also wanting to leave France and there was a long wait for the necessary papers. Meanwhile they settled in Marseille where Simone found work at the offices of the periodical *Cahier du Sud*. Another contributor described how she seemed to him in these months:

> A kind of bodyless bird, withdrawn inside itself, in a large black cloak down to her ankles that she never took off, still, silent...alien yet attentive, both observant and distant... Extremely ugly at first sight, thin ravaged face under her large black beret, thick ragged hair, only heavy black shoes to be seen under her ankle-length cloak...she would stare at you...her eyes very much to the fore as also her head and bust, centring on whomever she watched with her invasive shortsightedness, with an intensity and also a kind of questioning avidity that I've never encountered elsewhere...the eagerness in Weil's eyes was almost unbearable. In her presence all lies were out of the question...her denuding tearing and torn gaze...would grasp and render helpless the person she was looking at. (du Plessix Gray 2001)

The *Cahier du Sud* published an important essay on Homer's *Iliad*, written before she left Paris, two articles about the Albigensians, or Cathars, and an essay about the responsibility of French intellectuals for the debacle of 1940. Her anorexia persisted, and she had taken to sleeping on the bare floor of her room, as a further form of self-mortification. With her political views it is hardly surprising that Simone was questioned by the police several times, but she was able to continue to play a minor part in the Resistance movement. When she wanted to do some farm work she was put in touch with the writer Gustave Thibon, who lived in the village of Saint Marcel-sur-Ardèche, up the Rhône valley. Thibon was a philosopher and mystic, rather right-wing politically. He left a vivid impression of Simone's stay with him, one of the happiest periods in her unhappy life. He found her:

> prematurely bent and old-looking due to ascetism and illness…her magnificent eyes alone triumphing in this ship-wreck of beauty…it gave the impression of being face to face with an individual who was radically foreign to all my ways of thinking and feeling. She refused to make any concession whatever to the requirements and conventions of social life. (du Plessix Gray 2001)

She declined the bedroom Thibon offered her in his house as too comfortable, but accepted a half-ruined hut on the banks of the Rhône, where she could live just as she wished, her days filled with farmwork and housework, her evenings occupied with taking Thibon through Plato's *Phaedo* in Greek. 'She loved an argument,' he recalled, 'and went on *ad infinitum* in an inexorably monotonous voice.' By the end of her stay with him friends noticed a new gentleness, serenity and tenderness, although she still displayed a terrible preoccupation with herself.

That winter, back in Marseille, was the most fruitful period in her life as a writer. She worked on her journals with unprecedented intensity, preparing material that would find a place in the anthology *Waiting for God* that Thibon edited after her death. She also wrote the essays that were published as *Intimations of Christianity*. At the same time she became more active in the Resistance, without being much troubled by the police, although typically she once dropped a suitcase full of compromising material in the street, where it lay scattered around. When the time came to leave France she sailed with her parents to New York via Casablanca. Her brother André had also arrived in America with his wife, after various misadventures, and was teaching at Haverford College in Pennsylvania. Later he would move to the University of Chicago and end up at the Institute for Advanced Study, recognised as one of the truly great mathematicians of his generation.

There was a lull in Simone's literary work because although her spoken English was good her written English was not. When at last she was able to travel to England victory for the allied forces had just begun to seem possible. She arrived in London at the end of 1942, and lost no time in contacting the Free French. She felt depressed at the petty wrangling that was going on among the different factions. Her own ideas about the future of France were expressed in another book, *The Need for Roots*. Meanwhile she was denying herself enough food to remain alive, and her health was getting steadily worse. When she collapsed and was taken to hospital, she was diagnosed as having tuberculosis in both lungs; the doctors described her as the most difficult patient they had ever dealt with. The prognosis was poor and her will to live not strong. She wrote cheerful letters to her parents, still in New York, concealing from them the state of her health. She was moved to a sanatorium and a week later, on 24 August 1943, she died of heart failure, brought on by starvation and tuberculosis; the inquest recorded that she killed herself while the balance of mind was disturbed. Her parents could not face visiting her grave, but devoted the rest of their lives to the goal of preserving her work.

A human being so isolated, so self-deprecating, so desperate for community and affection is hardly imaginable, writes the psychologist Rosemary Dinnage (2004), who believes that Simone suffered from some degree of autism. Fitzgerald (2005) agrees. We know that Simone was hypersensitive and moody, as a child, indomitable, impossible to control, with an indescribable stubbornness. By the time she was four she disliked being kissed, even by her parents, and the rest of her life she displayed revulsion for most forms of physical contact. Her hands were unusually weak and maladroit. Also she wrote sloppily and slowly. She spoke in a high-pitched and monotonous tone of voice. She walked with long jerky steps and was notoriously clumsy, her piercing gaze, the clumsy clothing with which she covered her angular body, and above all a terrible preoccupation with herself. Both Simone and her brother André exhibited autistic traits; the indications are that these came from their father's side of the family. Disorders of the autistic spectrum are found much more often in men than in women, although this may be because women are better at compensating for some of their more noticeable features, being better at social relationships and less likely to exhibit narrow interest patterns.

Acknowledgment

The principal sources of information in this chapter are Fitzgerald (2005), du Plessix Gray (2001) and Petrement (1976).

CHAPTER SEVENTEEN

Alan Turing
(1912–1954)

Because his main interests were in things and ideas rather than in people, he was often alone. But he craved for affection and companionship – too strongly, perhaps, to make the first stages of friendship easy for him. (Robin Gandy)

People with Asperger's syndrome are attracted by mathematics and related subjects. I have already given a profile of the Indian mathematician Ramanujan (Chapter 13), and there are plenty of other examples of eminent mathematicians who were Asperger possibles. Our next profile is one of the most extraordinary. His life story tells us something about the difficulties that people with Asperger's have to overcome. Without it he might have had a happier life, but it is hard to believe he would have achieved so much.

Alan Mathison Turing was born on 23 June 1912, in the Paddington district of inner London. He had a brother John, three years older. The parents normally lived in Madras because their father Julius was in the Indian civil service, but the sons never saw India. Until they were ready for school they lived with a succession of foster parents, who they mostly disliked. Their father retired prematurely after being passed over for promotion. Later the elder son commented, 'I doubt whether I or Alan would have found my father an easy superior or subordinate for by all accounts he cared nothing for the hierarchy nor for his own future in the Indian civil service and spoke his mind regardless

of the consequences.' Their mother Ethel (née Stoney) came from an Anglo-Irish family that in the nineteenth century produced some distinguished physicists and engineers.

For tax reasons the parents settled in the French channel port of Dinard. The boys came over to stay with them at Christmas and Easter, while the parents came to take them on holiday in the summer. They were good-looking boys, John rather sharper, Alan more of a dreamer. According to his nanny, 'The thing that stands out most in my mind was his integrity and intelligence for a child so young as he then was, also you couldn't camouflage anything from him.' His self-sufficiency was apparent from an early age. Alan taught himself to read in about three weeks, and he was quick with figures. He would stop at every street lamp to check its serial number. He had no sense of left and right. The parents were determined their sons should be privately educated, although they could barely afford this. At preparatory school Alan had great difficulty with writing; his brain seemed scarcely coordinated with his hand. The teachers discouraged his absorbed interest in science, where he was largely self-taught. His mother, when he was nine, noticed a change of character in him, from being extremely vivacious, even mercurial, making friends with everyone, to being unsociable and dreamy. There is a wistful withdrawn expression in photographs of his ten-year-old face. Both sons took after their father in speaking their mind and applying their ideas with a determination punctuated by moments of recklessness.

In 1926 Alan entered Sherborne, a conventional boarding school for boys situated in Dorset. Although science was in the syllabus it had low prestige. Like most such schools the emphasis was on character and conduct, through a classical education supplemented by team sports. Alan stood out as odd, especially his shy, hesitant, high-pitched voice, not exactly stuttering but hesitating, as if waiting for some laborious process to translate his thoughts into human speech. One teacher said that Alan's handwriting was the worst he had ever seen. His teachers were impressed by his scientific abilities, but wanted to see more progress in other subjects; for example, he was bottom of the class in English and Latin. 'His mind seems rather chaotic at present and he finds great difficulty in expressing himself,' was one of the more enlightened comments in his school reports. Another said: 'He is the kind of boy who is bound to be rather a problem in any kind of school or community, being in some respects antisocial.'

Tired of tax exile the parents were now living in England. They wanted John to become a solicitor, but were not sure what career would suit Alan. He was fascinated by chemistry, always conducting experiments on his own, but mathematics seemed to be his strongest suit; later he said it gave him sexual pleasure. There was another boy at Sherborne named Christopher Morcom, older than Alan but small for his age and, as it turned out, suffering from tuberculosis. He was very able academically and shared Alan's passion for science. In the first of many homosexual affairs in his life, Alan fell in love with him. Christopher was about to sit the entrance scholarship for Cambridge and Alan resolved to do that too. They took the exam together, but Christopher was awarded a scholarship while Alan was not. Alan had premonitions that some disaster was about to strike his friend and, sure enough, Christopher was taken ill and died within a few days. Alan was heartbroken for years afterwards. Back at school Alan was now one of the senior boys, given some responsibility for discipline, as was customary, but he found it difficult to control the younger boys, who tended to make fun of him. In the Officers Training Corps he was made sergeant. Never lacking in physical stamina he began to excel in long-distance running. Later in life he ran marathons, until an injury to his hip curtailed his athletic ambitions.

When Turing tried again for a Cambridge scholarship, he was awarded one at King's, one of the more unconventional colleges, and in 1931 he went up to Cambridge to read mathematics. Although G.H. Hardy took an interest in him, his chief mentor was the topologist M.H.A. Newman, who was to be influential in the later stages of his career. Academically his main interests were mathematical logic and the theory of probability. He joined the college boat club and got drunk at at least one of its customary bibulous celebrations. He met a lot of interesting people, not all of them heterosexual, but socially he was not one of the elite. After graduation he was elected to a junior fellowship on the strength of a brilliant dissertation on probability, where characteristically he rediscovered one of the fundamental results of the subject. The fellowship, which had no explicit duties, provided a modest stipend with rooms and board; it lasted for three years, and was renewable for another three. His first major research paper, 'On computable numbers, with an application to the Entscheidungsprobleme', contained proof that there are mathematical problems which cannot be solved by any fixed and definite process, as in an automatic machine. It turned out that the Princeton logician Alonzo Church had also achieved this quite independently, using rather different methods, but Turing received full credit for his work, which aroused much interest.

At this time Princeton University was the Mecca for aspiring young mathematicians. Turing applied for a visiting fellowship, without success, but resolved to go there anyway. After a fruitful year working with Church, he decided to stay on and take a Princeton PhD before returning to Cambridge. He also learned to drive a car, no small achievement for one who was so ham-handed at operating anything mechanical, although he loved making things for himself. Back in Cambridge Turing had some contact with Ludwig Wittgenstein, but was not influenced by his philosophy. Instead Turing began thinking about machines for computing, where his grasp of mathematical logic led naturally to the design of what we know as the Turing machine, the basic idea of which underlies every computer we use today. Arguably it was an idea whose time had come, but it marked Turing's entry into the field to which he was to contribute so much.

We are now close to the outbreak of the Second World War. Turing had been interested in cryptanalysis at school but now he started to work on it with characteristic vigour. The British government had established a code and cipher school, which was being relocated to Bletchley Park, midway between Oxford and Cambridge. Turing became involved with the work being carried out there, and once war broke out he was appointed by the Foreign Office as chief cryptanalyst. At Bletchley he led an able group of mathematicians and others who were trying to break the various codes used by the enemy. Their main task was to understand the workings of the German Enigma machine, and to decode military and naval messages as they were intercepted. Turing became the driving force behind this work, which was not very sophisticated mathematically, more a long slog using intelligence and elementary mathematics. Towards the end of the war Turing was sent to America for a time as a kind of liaison officer: his mother was very proud of him for this. However, his habit of taking any instructions he was given quite literally led to various kinds of trouble with the security-conscious Americans.

At one stage Turing decided he would like to get married, and formed an attachment with a junior member of the Bletchley staff. After explaining about his homosexual inclinations he proposed to her, and she accepted, but before long he changed his mind. Fortunately the authorities were unaware of Turing's sexual orientation, said one Bletchley veteran, or Britain might have lost the war.

There are many stories about Turing's eccentric behaviour, told by those who knew him at Bletchley. For example, he wanted to protect his modest savings from expropriation, as much by the British government as by the enemy. So he invested in two bars of silver and buried them in a nearby wood. He wrote down the precise location, translated that into code, and buried that in another location. However, he was never able to find the silver again. Another story tells how he enrolled in the Home Guard with the aim of learning how to use a rifle. Once he had become a good shot he ceased to attend parades. When told this was an offence under military law he pointed out that, on the enrolment form, he had answered 'No' to the question: 'Do you understand that you will be liable to military law?' This had passed unnoticed.

Turing had an enthusiasm and humour which made him a generous and lovable personality and won him many friends, not least among children. One of his colleagues was the topologist Peter Hilton, who recalled:

> There was always a sense of this immense power and of his ability to tackle every problem, and always from first principles. I mean he not only did a lot of theoretical work, but he actually designed machines to help in the solution of problems and with all the electrical circuitry that would be involved as well. He always tackled the whole problem and never ran away from a calculation. If it was a question of knowing how something would in fact behave in practice, he would do all the numerical calculations as well. We were all very much inspired by him, his interest in the work but the simultaneous interest in almost everything else…and he was a delightful person to work with. He had great patience with those who were not as gifted as himself. I remember he always gave me great encouragement whenever I did anything which was at all noteworthy. And we were very very fond of him. It was pure joy to achieve something new and show him, and have him grunt, gasp, brush back his hair, and exclaim, stabbing with his fingers; I see! I see! (Newman 1955)

The war years were perhaps the happiest of Turing's life, but the loss to science of what should have been six of his most fruitful years of research was regrettable. After the war he returned to Cambridge for a short while, still on his Junior Fellowship. No one was closer to Turing than his research student Robin Gandy, who became reader in mathematical logic at Oxford and even adopted some of Turing's mannerisms. Turing was still youthful in appearance with a roguish charm, piercing blue eyes, luxuriant eye-lashes and a soft-contoured nose. He was not short of sexual partners, to one of whom he remarked, 'I have more contact with this bed than with other people.' His father died, at the age of seventy-three, after some years of poor health. In research Turing was thinking about intelligent machinery, what we now call artificial intelligence, and wanted to get his hands on computers again. He worked at the National Physical Laboratory for a time, as a senior principal scientific officer in the mathematical division, developing a working pilot model of what was called the Automatic Computing Engine.

After the war Newman, Turing's mentor at Cambridge and colleague at Bletchley, was appointed to a chair at Manchester University, and started building up a mathematics department which on a small scale came to rival the one at Cambridge. Newman appreciated the potential of computers as well as anyone, and if he lacked Turing's emotional thrust towards 'building a brain', and the experience of assembling components himself, he compensated with greater skill in the art of the possible. Both Newman and Turing were particularly interested in the possibility of using computers on more intellectual tasks, such as playing a game of chess, or solving problems in pure mathematics. In his seminal 1950 paper 'Computing and Intelligence', Turing examined the arguments for and against the view that machines might be said to think. He suggested that machines can learn and may eventually compete with men in all purely intellectual fields.

When Newman recruited Turing, he was well aware that he would be something of a misfit. Turing always preferred to work on his own. There were those like Hilton, another Newman recruit, who appreciated Turing's creative anarchy, but other colleagues found him very difficult. One of them commented on his rather frightening attention to anything said to him; he took everything so seriously, and would be puzzling out its implications for days afterwards. In replying to a question he was liable to go on for hours about it until he would suddenly stop and leave without a word. At first he lived in lodgings near the university but later bought a house in Wilmslow, a middle-class suburb further out on the edge of open country. Knowing his loneliness, the Newmans made every effort to give Turing some social life, but most people were put off by his off-hand manners.

Newman's wife, the writer Lyn Irvine, commented on his long silences, which ended with a shrill stammer and a crowing laugh which told upon the nerves. She also noticed how he tended to avoid eye contact; a strategy adopted by people with Asperger's.

Turing used to make frequent short visits to Cambridge where he was able to maintain contact with his circle of gay friends. To be close to him it was essential to accept him as a homosexual; he never tried to conceal it. Acts of gross indecency, as they were called, were severely punished in the courts, and homosexuals were often the victims of blackmail. One day Turing picked up a nineteen-year-old youth in Manchester and brought him back to spend the night. This happened several times and after one such visit Turing found that some of his property was missing. Naively he reported this to the police, who soon became more interested in the homosexual angle than the theft. He was charged with gross indecency, to which he pleaded guilty, but as a first offender was placed on probation on condition that he received medical treatment from a suitably qualified medical practitioner. The new oestrogen treatment he received was designed to make him impotent, at least temporarily. The alternative was a prison sentence.

By this time Turing had turned forty. His contributions to research had resulted in his being elected to the Royal Society in 1951. After some years of indecision he found, in his chemical theory of growth and form, a scheme that gave fullest scope to his rare combination of abilities, as a mathematical analyst with a flair for machine computing, and a natural philosopher full of bold original ideas. Naturally he was depressed by the humiliating treatment he was receiving. After the year of probation he seemed to carry on much as before. He made a new will, which may or may not be significant. Turing died on 7 June 1954, from cyanide poisoning. He had been playing around with some chemicals, as he often did, including potassium cyanide. The apple he always ate before going to bed may have been contaminated by it. His mother believed it was an accident but the coroner returned a verdict of suicide. He left behind a mass of papers, mainly concerned with morphogenesis, but he was not on the verge of an epoch-making discovery. As Newman wrote in his biographical memoir, his untimely death deprived mathematics and science of a great original mind at the height of his power.

O'Connell and Fitzgerald (2003) believe that Turing certainly meets the criteria for Asperger's syndrome. As well as the patterns of behaviour already described, there was much else. For example, he cared little for his personal appearance at any stage in his life. He rarely bothered to shave, his nails were stuffed with dirt, and his clothes were a mass of creases. There seems no doubt that his Asperger's syndrome came from his father's side of the family. Turing's mother (who preferred to be called by her second name of Sara rather than Ethel) survived him and wrote the memoir, which appeared in 1959. It contains disappointingly little in it about her son's early years, and she never understood his professional work at all. In many respects he was a stranger to her; if she knew about his sex life, she didn't care to write about it. What he had been doing at Bletchley was still hush-hush, but as his colleague Jack Good remarked: 'I won't say that what he did there made us win the war, but I daresay we might have lost it without him.' There have been persistent rumours that he was involved in cybernetic research involving human subjects during the war; previously secret documents now released confirm that he underwent a series of state-directed procedures near the end of his life but do not explain their nature.

Acknowledgment

The principal sources of information in this chapter are Hodges (1983), O'Connell and Fitzgerald (2003) and Turing (1959).

CHAPTER EIGHTEEN

Patricia Highsmith (1921–1995)

Hatred interested her more than love, the skewed more than the normal, the defeated more than the successful. (William Trevor)

There were, of course, writers with strong indications of Asperger's syndrome after Jonathan Swift, such as the English story-teller Charles Ludwidge Dodgson (Lewis Carroll) and the Irish poet William Butler Yeats, whose cases are discussed by Fitzgerald (2004). However, it is more difficult to find *female* writers who were Asperger possibles. The English novelist Jane Austen and the American poet Emily Dickinson have been suggested but the available evidence seems weak. A better example is the American novelist Patricia Highsmith, who described herself as a writer of suspense fiction. Her best-known books are *Strangers on a Train* and the Ripley novels. There is something rather disturbing about most of her stories. Although not exactly autobiographical, they were often inspired by her own experiences.

Patricia Plangman, as she was called in her earlier years, was born in Fort Worth, Texas, on 19 January 1921. Only nine days previously her mother, Mary Coates Plangman, and father, Jay Bernard Plangman, had divorced, after a marriage that had lasted just eighteen months. Patricia did not meet her natural father until she was twelve; apparently he had not wanted his former wife to have a baby and urged that she have an abortion. Mary had shown an early talent for drawing

From Wilson, A. (2003) *Beautiful Shadow: A Life of Patricia Highsmith*. London: Bloomsbury Publishing

and painting and hoped to become a fashion illustrator. She was very strong-willed and career-minded. Stanley Highsmith, who became her second husband, was a commercial artist who was five years younger than Mary and also lived in Fort Worth; they married when Patricia was three. He is said to have been an extremely quiet man, with a dry sense of humour. Patricia, an only child, was very close to her mother and rejected her stepfather.

When she was six the family moved to New York for a time, in search of better job opportunities, and Patricia began her school education. By this time she had become aware that her sexual orientation was not normal; that she was a boy in the body of a girl. When she was fourteen her mother had asked her if she was a lesbian. Looking back on her childhood, towards the end of her life, she thought she might have been sexually abused between the ages of four or five, although she had no clear recollection of this. After a year in New York the family moved back to Fort Worth and then returned to New York a year later. Her mother and stepfather were quarrelling constantly. Mary took Patricia back to Fort Worth, leaving Stanley behind; then Stanley came and took Mary back to New York, leaving Patricia with her grandmother. Patricia felt rejected, and described this as the saddest year of her life. It was then that she met her real father for the first time, but they did not become at all close. Patricia yearned for Mary, and in 1934 she rejoined her mother and stepfather in New York, where they were continuing to have endless rows.

When she graduated from high school she had already made up her mind to become a writer. She registered for the four-year course in English Literature at Barnard College, a part of Columbia University reserved for women. Her creative instinct began to find expression when she became deputy editor of the college magazine. Contemporaries described her as difficult to know; a private person who gave nothing away. At home Patricia began to realise that it was her mother that was the problem, not her stepfather, but still she remained close to her mother. Because she had never been formally adopted by her stepfather, it became necessary to legalise the position, so that Patricia had to grit her teeth and swear that her, her mother and her stepfather had lived together as a closely knit family for twenty-one years.

After graduating from Barnard, Highsmith worked for various magazines while writing short stories, usually creepy and homoerotic. She found she could only get rid of her nightmares by writing. She started work on her first really successful book, *Strangers on a Train*, which she finished at Yaddo, the elite colony of artists and writers in upstate New York, in the summer of 1948. Then she took a course of psychoanalysis, trying in vain to modify her sexual orientation. She seemed to be attracted to women who were somewhat androgynous. Highsmith had no desire to become regarded as a lesbian writer; when her next major work, *The Price of Salt*, was successful she used a pseudonym because it had a lesbian theme. This was followed by the first of the novels which feature the pleasure-loving amateur villain Tom Ripley. She was compared to Georges Simenon, another author who had transformed the ordinary crime novel into something that could be regarded as serious literature.

During the 1950s and 1960s, the most fruitful period of her career, Highsmith was mainly living in Europe. She came to dislike her homeland, partly because her books were so much less successful there, and this in turn may have been affected by her support for the

Palestinian cause rather than the Israeli one. After a period in England she settled in France, in the Fontainebleau area south of Paris. Although she stayed for thirteen years, her knowledge of the French language remained primitive and she had difficulty adjusting herself to French ways, especially French cuisine. She had been drinking heavily for years but now her behaviour was becoming quite peculiar, as visitors soon discovered. She claimed to be a lover of fine food, but what she served up to guests was unappetising, and to be a keen gardener, but the piece of land around her house was totally neglected. She was crazy about her Siamese cats, and spoke to them in a special language. She developed a great passion for snails, and used to carry a hundred or so of them around with her, feeding them on lettuce. She enjoyed shocking people. Living in Europe did not shield her from her mother's attentions. Once Highsmith brought Mary to France but discovered that her mother was impersonating her, for example giving interviews to journalists in her name. Mary kept sending her vicious letters and it became clear that she had mental problems. When her house in Fort Worth caught fire due to her carelessness, she was moved to a retirement home where she spent the rest of her unhappy life.

Highsmith had very definite ideas about what she did and did not like. Likes included Bach's *St Matthew Passion*, old clothes, sneakers, absence of noise, Mexican food, fountain pens, Swiss army knives, weekends without any social commitments, Kafka and being alone. Dislikes included the music of Sibelius, the art of Leger, live concerts, four-course meals, television sets, the Begin-Sharon regime, loud-mouthed people and those who borrow money, being recognised by strangers in the street, fascists and burglars.

After thirteen years as a French resident Highsmith was starting to attract the attention of the tax authorities. When they came one day to search her house she reacted by moving to Switzerland, where she bought an unattractive old house in the Ticino, without any outlook. Visitors were appalled by her living conditions. Eventually she bought some land nearby and had a fine modern house built, with lovely views over the valley below and the mountains beyond. It was at the Casa Highsmith that she spent the final years of her life.

In adolescence Highsmith had been for a time anorexic. Later in life she experienced periods of depression. To boost her spirits she decided to take up oil-painting. One friend gave her a set of oils for her seventieth birthday and another volunteered to show her how to paint with them, but 'it was very difficult to teach her, to tell her anything. She was shy, hard-headed and she had her own ideas.' Around the age of sixty Highsmith had undergone surgery for lung cancer, after which she gave up smoking, although assured that the cancer was unrelated to that. Increasingly she worried about her health and in 1991, after her mother's death, she began to prepare for her own. She drew up a will leaving almost everything to Yaddo. Expecting that the University of Texas would be interested in acquiring her literary papers she asked how much they would be willing to pay. Their offer was, she thought, insultingly low, so she asked her executors to negotiate a sale to the Swiss Literary Archives in Bern instead. She died of aplastic anaemia on 4 February 1995.

Highsmith was markedly masculine in appearance, and something of a man-hater, a kind of female chauvinist. Not surprisingly the most negative opinion of her comes from a man:

> I'm an enthusiast by nature, an optimist and a generally upbeat sort of person but she was one of the most odious people I've ever met. She was mean, unkindly, unfriendly and cold, and never missed an opportunity to be nasty. She was pretty good-looking when she was younger but she was ugly later in life. I think a lot of that ugliness – that anger and that hatred, hatred of almost everything and anyone – came from inside.

Women found her rather different. In Switzerland one of her neighbours said, 'The only thing I didn't like about her was the fact that when you went to greet her, she never held your hand. She didn't know how to react; she didn't like to breathe other people's air.' Another said, 'She was one of the most sensitive, vulnerable and insecure people I've ever met.' Vivien de Bernardi, an educational therapist, wrote:

> Although she wrote about violence she was a very gentle person.
> I loved being with her because there was this sense of quiet... I
> didn't like to be with her when other people were around
> because she behaved like an unruly child, saying the first thing
> that popped into her head. It was as if she didn't seem to have
> any inner control mechanisms. She was incapable of not saying
> what was in her mind. With hindsight I think that Pat could have
> had a form of high-functioning Asperger's syndrome. She had a
> lot of typical traits. She had a terrible sense of direction. She was
> hypersensitive to sound and had these communication difficul-
> ties. Most of us screen certain things, but she would spit out
> everything she thought. She was not aware of the nuances of
> conversation and she didn't realize when she had hurt other
> people. (Wilson 2003)

There were other Asperger features in Highsmith's behaviour. There
was motor clumsiness: gaucherie and lack of grace in her movements.
There was her orderliness. 'If you moved an ashtray in one of her
houses, she would immediately put it back in the same place.' She was
obsessive about cleanliness. 'In the supermarket she was overwhelmed
by sensory stimulation,' said a friend. 'There were too many people
and too much noise and she just could not handle it.'

If Vivien de Bernardi is right about Highsmith having Asperger's,
we might look for signs of the disorder among her ancestors. We know
too little of her father, who was of German stock, but on her mother's
side there are indications. Highsmith's maternal grandparents were
Daniel and Willie Mae Coates. Daniel's family were noted for having
large feet and hands, a physical characteristic she inherited. However,
it is Willie Mae who might be most relevant. She was quite small, had a
'head of stone', was 'amazingly strong-willed' and opinionated. She
was very much her own woman; Mary, her only daughter, took after
her, and Highsmith was strongly influenced by both of them.

Acknowledgment

The principal source of information in this chapter is Wilson (2003).

CHAPTER NINETEEN

Andy Warhol (1928–1987)

If you want to know all about Andy Warhol, just look at the surface of my paintings and films and me and there I am. There's nothing behind it. (Andy Warhol 1975)

Andy Warhol was enormously successful as a commercial artist in New York in the 1950s. In 1960 he began making paintings based on mass-produced images such as newspaper advertisements and comic strips. His paintings of Campbell's soup cans were such a sensational success that Warhol soon found himself the most famous and controversial figure in American Pop Art. His celebrity, carefully cultivated by himself, came as much from his lifestyle as from his work. According to Fitzgerald (2005) the evidence for Asperger's syndrome is very strong. His remark 'I feel I'm from another planet' is common among people with the syndrome.

Andrew Warhola, as he was called as a child, was born on 6 August 1928, in the industrial city of Pittsburgh, Pennsylvania. His parents came from Ruthenia when it was still part of Austro-Hungary. His hard-working father, Ondrej Warhola, had emigrated to the United States, where he worked in coal mining for some years, later as a builder's labourer. Just before the First World War Ondrej returned to his homeland to find a wife, and married Julia Zavacky.

Once the war was over Julia was able to join Ondrej in America. They had three children, Paul in 1922, John three years later, and then

Andrew in 1928. The parents were devout Uniate Catholics; the Church was the centre of all Ruthenian social activity. Since Julia refused to learn English, the language used at home was a mixture of Hungarian and Ukrainian. Andy's artistic gifts came from her; she was a folk artist who liked to make small carvings and paint designs on household utensils, and she was also musical. He also took after her in his tendency to cry easily, his desire to perform, his belief in destiny and magic, his penchant for death and disaster, and his ability to mythologise everything that happened to him. He obscured his childhood in myth once he became famous. It seems likely that the syndrome came from her side of the family.

Andy was a happy-go-lucky boy. His brother Paul said he was full of mischief. He would learn rude words from other boys and then repeat them in the most inappropriate social settings, so his family often locked him out of the house. One of his schoolteachers remembered him as 'a towhead with light eyes, very quiet, not at all outgoing, and he was real good at drawing'. Like many other children who grew up in poor neighbourhoods, he caught rheumatic fever, which can affect the central nervous system. His skin suffered a permanent loss of pigmentation, which gave him a ghostly appearance, except for an embarrassing red patch on his bulbous nose. His mother took special care of her youngest son; she knew just what he needed. 'I used to have the same lunch every day for twenty years I guess,' he recalled, 'the same thing over and over again.' His lunch was always Campbell's soup.

Although Pittsburgh was an industrial city, it was an excellent place to study art. The public school system specialised in teaching art and had a number of innovative and dedicated instructors who were responsible for giving Andy not only a solid grounding in the field but also the inspiration to see art as a way of life. The interest of the Pittsburgh elite in art led them to sponsor art competitions, art centres and Saturday morning art classes for talented children at the Carnegie Museum. Joseph Fitzpatrick, one of the local artists who taught at these classes, said afterwards that Andy was magnificently talented:

Personally he was not attractive, a little bit obnoxious. He had no consideration for other people, he was socially inept at the time and showed little or no appreciation for anything. He was not pleasant with members of his class or with any of the people with whom he associated. But he did seem to have a goal from the very start. You weren't conscious of what it was, but he stayed right with it. (Bockris 1989)

Warhol became a protégé of this artist, who later commented that 'he created his repertoire of behaviour and appearance to gain attention. He seemed to be extremely keen on knowing people, and he knew exactly what to do to get the attention he outwardly seemed to avoid.'

One of his classmates at high school recalled: 'He wasn't one to show off at all. In fact he was very close with his personal life. He wasn't part of any cliques, he sort of got left out, but he wasn't in the art club because he was so superior to the rest of us.' Another said:

He was oddball-looking but not oddball as a person, and he didn't dress outlandishly. He often wore a favourite sweater vest with the sleeves of his shirt rolled up and like almost everyone else he wore saddle shoes. But he had that white hair which he wore in bangs or swept back. Most of the other boys wore crew cuts, and sometimes they made fun of him – they called him the albino. (Bockris 1989)

His art teacher recalled that 'he was pale, he had a sallow complexion with high cheekbones and washed out tannish hair that was almost the colour of his skin'. Another teacher described him as 'quiet, sensitive, intense. In my classes he seemed to pal with no one, but to become immersed in his work. He was in no way a problem, but hard to know personally.'

Andy's father was determined that he should go to college. After his death Andy set out to achieve this, becoming much more disciplined and self-directed in his work. His brother John said Andy was determined as a child and so serious and quiet. 'I thought he was going to be a priest [Andy was a regular churchgoer all his life] but I think that's when he started planning being an artist.' His sister-in-law recalled:

when Andy came home from school he would go straight to his room and work. Dinner would be ready and you could hear his mother yelling for him to come down and eat. Sometimes she would take food up to him. When he did come down and eat with us he never had much to say and when he did talk it was always about his work and nobody paid too much attention. He was really wrapped up in his work. He was more serious than most of us were, but that didn't mean he didn't have fun. (Bockris 1989)

During his senior year at high school, Andy had been accepted by both the University of Pittsburgh and the Carnegie Institute of Technology. He chose the latter because it offered an excellent well-rounded art education. 'Andy told me he had been accepted,' his brother John recalled, 'but he wasn't excited about it. Andy wasn't the sort of person who really showed his expression. He did tell me he was glad but that was about it.' At first his mother paid the fees from her savings. The academic standards at Carnegie Tech were high, the courses were competitive, and hard work was stressed. Later his class-mates would say they knew he was a genius but at the time he was regarded as the class baby, a born loser. One of his teachers remembered him as a small thin boy who had a great talent for avoiding personal contact. He had trouble with some of his art classes, because he was already set in his unconventional ways, but his main problem was a course on thought and expression, in which students attended plays staged by the drama department or read books and then discussed their reactions and wrote interpretative essays. Andy never spoke in this class and was incapable of forming his thoughts coherently in writing. Two of his classmates helped him but the trouble was his inability to put his thoughts into literate English. He had supporters among the faculty both because he was obviously extremely talented and because he was still very young-looking, but at the end of the first year he was suspended and told to take summer school to make up his deficiencies. To pay for this he got a job with his brother Paul delivering groceries.

Warhol graduated from Carnegie Tech in 1949. By this time he was a hero to many of the other art students. The previous year he had taken the first step in his art career by taking a part-time job working on the window displays for the premier department store in Pittsburgh. He earned enough doing this to go to New York and show his pictorial work to the fashion magazines. While he was there he went to the Museum of Modern Art and saw for the first time original work by Pablo Picasso, Henri Matisse and other Post-Impressionists. He resolved to return when he graduated.

In New York, the next year, he began living in a communal apartment. Someone who remembered him there said that:

> although he may have been nineteen at the time he seemed even younger. And so shy – he hardly spoke at all. One of the girls in the apartment got so mad at Andy for not talking to her she threw an egg at him and hit him on the head with it. (Bockris 1989)

However, Andy was getting on quite well as an illustrator and commercial artist. It was at this point he changed his name to Andy Warhol. 'Andy was one of the plainest boys I've ever seen in my life,' said someone who knew him then, 'a pimply-faced adolescent with a deformed bulbous nose that was always inflamed. He looked right off the boat. He was very poorly dressed and carried a torn portfolio under his arm.' He became infatuated with the famous writer Truman Capote, who later recalled:

> Andy used to stand outside the building where I lived and hang around waiting to see me come in or go out. He seemed to be one of those hopeless people you just know nothing's ever going to happen to... A hopeless born loser, the loneliest and most friendless person I'd ever seen in my life. (Bockris 1989)

In 1952 Andy's mother Julia unexpectedly came to live with him, believing he was incapable of looking after himself properly. She said she would only stay until he found a nice girl and got married. Although embarrassed by her arrival at first, he realised it fitted with the poor-little-boy persona he was cultivating at the time. They rented an apartment where there was hardly any furniture, just a couple of mattresses on the floor, and paintings stacked around the walls. A tribe of Siamese cats shared it with them. 'Julia was the source of the tenacity and gentleness and down-to-earth resilience that were at the core of Andy's character,' commented the art historian John Richardson. 'Narrow-minded and uneducated she may have been but Julia struck those who met her as humorous, mischievous and shrewd – like her son. Underneath her naive peasant exterior was the only person in Andy's life who was as complex, manipulative and powerful as he was.' Their mutual dependence, along with his acute self-consciousness, made other relationships nearly impossible.

People who knew him then remember him as inarticulate, totally non-verbal, whimsical, fey, sweet and charming, but painfully shy. Despite his shyness, Warhol rapidly became successful – he worked for the top New York department stores and the most prestigious glossy magazines; his speciality was drawing footwear. Cooperative, prompt and professional, he was soon earning $100,000 a year and in 1957 was awarded the medal of the Art Director's Club for his work as a freelance commercial illustrator. His skill at presenting himself was extraordinary. He would show up at the offices of *Vogue* or *Harper's Bazaar* looking like some undernourished street urchin in his torn chinos and dirty sneakers – 'Raggedy Andy', they called him. The editors and art directors found him irresistible. He was like an innocent child; he had a childlike quality that fascinated people.

Although in the world of commercial art Warhol was already something of a star, his ambition was to be recognised in the world of fine art as well. He exhibited regularly in the late 1950s, mainly selections from his bread-and-butter work, but his paintings aroused little critical attention. Some of them were distinctly homosexual in theme. Warhol had been frequenting gay society for some years, and in 1954 he experienced his first real love affair. Charles Lisanby was a wealthy socialite from Kentucky who took him to chic parties where Warhol would sit in a corner, not saying a word. According to Lisanby, 'Warhol had an enormous inferiority complex. He told me he was from another planet – he didn't know how he got here. People thought he was dumb. He was anything but dumb. He was more brilliant than he ever knew.' Lisanby took Warhol on a world tour but when they got back to

New York he was shocked when Warhol walked out on him, without a word, the moment they cleared customs.

Warhol, now approaching thirty, found his appearance was putting off some of the gay youths he was attracted to. The skin condition he acquired in childhood was part of the problem. Cosmetic surgery to deal with the porous red skin on his nose had not been a success. Because he was becoming bald he started to wear a hat, indoors and out. The little-boy image had served him well so far but it was time to try a new persona. He bought some silver-blond wigs that he wore uncombed and slightly askew, and he began to wear dark glasses all the time. He also started to change the way he spoke, mumbling monosyllabic, often incoherent replies to questions, and he acquired some new obsessions, for example he would play the same Pop record over and over again, until he 'understood what it meant'.

Warhol also became involved with an avant-garde theatre group working on the Lower East Side for whom he designed sets. It is probably through this group that he became acquainted with Bertolt Brecht's theory of alienation – the idea that the work of art deliberately distances the spectator and invites judgement, rather than identification with what is shown. In 1960 he made a series of paintings based on newspapers and fragments of comic strips – the images he selected were photographed, projected onto canvas and filled in by hand. These works were shown as window decorations at the Bonwit Teller store on Fifty-seventh street in April 1961, following a precedent set by Robert Rauchenberg and Jasper Johns. But no established gallery would accept them, despite the fact that Pop imagery was beginning to surface regularly in art. Part of the problem was that Roy Lichtenstein was producing work that looked superficially similar, but was clearly more accomplished and better presented.

Warhol felt that he had reached an impasse – until, at the joking suggestion of a friend, he made his first paintings of dollar bills and Campbell soup cans, objects so familiar that people had ceased to notice what they looked like. At first he painted the images freehand, but soon, as literalism was the aim, it seemed logical to silk-screen them on to canvas. The soup cans were quickly followed by pictures of Coca Cola bottles, portraits from photographic originals of Marilyn

Monroe, Elvis Presley, Elizabeth Taylor and other celebrities – these were ironic allusions to the cult of the star that was an important part of the new Pop mythology. The pictures of Campbell soup cans were exhibited in the summer of 1962 in Los Angeles, and in the autumn of the same year Warhol had a show at the Stable Gallery in New York. The timing was exactly right, and the exhibition caused a sensation.

He now took a studio on East Forty-seventh street, which he named The Factory, and began to mass-produce silk-screened paintings with the aid of a crowd of helpers and hangers on, described as 'cultural space-debris, drifting fragments from a variety of sixties subcultures'. New subjects were found – a series of car crashes, images of the electric chair. In 1963 he started to make films. At first these were extremely primitive, and their main theme seemed to be boredom. The camera was simply left to stare at an object or person, sometimes for hours on end. As Warhol said:

> I like boring things. When you just sit and look out of a window, that's enjoyable. It takes up time. Yeah. Really. You see people looking out of the window all the time, I do. If you're not looking out of a window, you're sitting in a shop in the street. My films are just a way of taking up time. (Bockris 1989)

Soon, however, they became rather more than that – they developed into a voyeuristic examination of the people with whom Warhol now surrounded himself. They included runaway girls from good families, like the tragic Edie Sedgwick, who was to die of a drug overdose; aspiring New York socialites, like Baby Jane Holzer; transvestites, hustlers and addicts. They acted out their traumas and fantasies in the presence of their seemingly passive host. 'I don't know where the artificial stops and the real begins,' Warhol once declared. 'With film you just turn on the camera and photograph something. I leave the camera running until it runs out of film, because that way I can catch somebody being themselves.'

He now made another change in the way he looked. He had been frequenting sado-masochistic clubs, as a voyeur rather than active participant. He was always curious about what other people did sexually, although he would say: 'Oh, you're better off putting all your energy into your work.' He acquired a taste for delinquents who were much younger than he was. In his new persona Warhol dressed in a muscle-man's black leather jacket, tight black jeans, T-shirt, high-heeled boots and, of course, the silver wig and dark glasses. He looked clean, hard and arrogant. He hardly ever laughed. He rarely spoke in public, and when he did it was in a new disembodied voice, laced with several layers of sarcasm and contempt, and tended to repeat single words over and over again. Critic Peter York said: 'The absolute flatness [of his voice], the affectlessness, meant you couldn't see behind it at all' (York, cited in Fitzgerald 2005). Undoubtedly he displayed peculiarities of speech and language.

By the mid-1960s Warhol was surrounded by an extraordinary atmosphere of hysteria. His first retrospective exhibition, held in 1965 at the University of Pennsylvania Institute of Contemporary Art, generated a near riot at its opening, as guests pressed close to the hero of the occasion. Warhol and Edie Sedgwick had to be smuggled out of a side door, as were many of the exhibits to save them from damage. By this time Warhol had already moved to a more prestigious New York art gallery where he exhibited two series of paintings. One of these pictures was of *Flowers*, based on a photograph he had discovered in a women's magazine; it had won first prize in a contest for the best picture taken by a housewife. The Factory produced over nine hundred *Flowers* in all sizes. In 1966 Warhol announced his retirement from painting on the grounds that it was no longer interesting.

He now turned to rock music – the Velvet Underground band, which he started, gave its first performance, in a setting provided by a mixed-media show he directed. In June 1968 he became the victim of his self-created legend. He was shot and critically injured by a young lesbian anarchist named Valerie Solanas, who had appeared briefly in his film *Bikeboy*. Six months previously she had founded an organization with the acronym SCUM – the Society for Cutting Up Men – of which she was sole member. Warhol was the particular male on whom she chose to vent her anger. However, he survived and later said it was a pity the camera wasn't running when the attack took place. In 1969 he began to publish a monthly tabloid that chronicled the careers and lifestyles of a wide range of celebrities, mainly in the entertainment, art and fashion worlds. Soon afterwards his mother, who was in poor health, returned to Pittsburgh; when she died in 1972 he did not attend her funeral.

Though he never entirely gave up painting, Warhol's reputation rests on the work he did before he was shot. It is often said that this traumatic event soured him, driving him towards more cynical modes of art making. He continued, sometimes under protest, to produce vast quantities of images, in intervals snatched from other, more fascinating but less reliably lucrative activities. Despite the apparent cynicism of his attitudes, Warhol was still highly regarded by the international visual arts establishment. In 1981, for example, he was the only American Pop artist to be included in the exhibition *A New Spirit in Painting*, held at the Royal Academy in London.

Warhol was one of the most enthusiastic partygoers of his time, as is amply recorded in the diaries published after his death. His over-active social life was relentlessly photographed by the paparazzi. Although he liked to mix with the famous, his followers included undesirables. Warhol liked to give the idea that he took a paternal interest in them but, when one jumped from a fifth-floor window when high on amphetamines, he was heard complaining that he should have been forewarned so that he could have filmed it. Although apparently careless about money, in some ways he was building up a fortune through shrewd investment in real estate. He spent a lot of his time buying and selling antiques and collecting all kinds of other things, such as cookie jars, sometimes in vast quantities.

At the end of 1975 Warhol had moved into a six-storey 1911 Georgian-style mansion in the heart of the Upper East Side, with wide stairways and large, light open rooms. For years he had been collecting Art Deco furniture; now he changed to American Empire furniture. He said the antiques made him feel rich. The elegant staterooms were increasingly used just for storage; meals were taken in the kitchen. He kept most of the rooms locked. He would walk through the house every morning before he left, open the door of each room with a key, peer in, then relock it. At night when he came home he would unlock each door, turn the light on, peer in, lock up again, and only then go to bed.

For some time Warhol had been suffering from stomach pains. When he finally agreed to surgery it had become an emergency. The operation was successful but the post-operative care was lax, and Warhol died in hospital on 22 February 1987. The immensely successful sale at auction of his vast collections (everything from fine furniture to cookie jars, mostly never unpacked) proved how successfully he had established himself in the popular imagination. He left a fortune estimated at $100,000,000, most of which went to create an arts charity, the Andy Warhol Foundation for the Visual Arts. In 1994 a museum dedicated to his work opened in his hometown of Pittsburgh. The immediacy of fame was what mattered to him, not the judgement of posterity.

Those who have a disorder on the autism spectrum themselves are often interested in identifying others who have one. The composer Ian Stewart, in a recent lecture at the National Autistic Society in London, made out the case for Warhol having had some form of autism, and this is supported by Ratey and Johnson (1997). Stewart explained that what first convinced him was the chapter 'Underwear Power' Warhol wrote in 1975. 'I think underwear must be especially problematic for people who are autistic,' Stewart remarked, 'because I have to get exactly the same type from the same high street shop year in year out and I'm sure green underwear feels different from other colours.' For Warhol, it was necessary to examine even the label on the packaging to make sure nothing had changed, such as the washing instructions. Stewart goes on to address the question of how autism affected Warhol's art:

> He was, of course, an exceptional draughtsman, one of the skills often found in people with autism... He is usually credited with introducing multiple versions of the same images in a grid pattern into art... Such patterns are more likely to register and be of interest to someone who is autistic.

We do not have to look far to find other evidence that Warhol may have had the syndrome. At school he showed a great talent for avoiding personal contact. 'He had no consideration for other people. He lacked all the amenities. He was socially inept at the time and showed little or no appreciation for anything.' 'He never had much to say and when he did talk it was always about his work. He was really wrapped up in his work.' The absolute flatness of his voice, his peculiar locutions and his inability to process human speech correctly are also indications. He cringed from physical contact. The obsessive playing of gramophone records and the collecting of furniture and objects such as cookie jars are also significant, likewise his obsessive archival activities, in which he documented his 'wrongness'. Biographers mention his tendency to establish routines, such as the regular morning and evening rounds of his collections. Far from attempting to conceal such characteristic patterns of behaviour, he started to exaggerate and exploit them; some of his followers copied what he did. Warhol (1975) describes himself as a loner: 'I wasn't close to anyone, I felt left out.' 'Every single thing I do looks strange,' he said. 'I have such a strange walk and a strange look... What's wrong with me?' He enumerated what he saw in the mirror:

> Nothing is missing. It's all there. The affectless gaze. The diffracted grace...the bored languor, the wasted pallor...the chic freakiness, the basically passive astonishment...the glamour rooted in despair, the self-admiring carelessness, the perfected otherness, the shadowy, voyeuristic, vaguely sinister aura ...nothing is missing. I'm everything my scrapbook says I am. (Warhol 1975)

Acknowledgment

The principal sources of information in this chapter are Bockris (1989), Bourdon (1989), Cooke (1999), Fitzgerald (2005), Hackett (1989) and Warhol (1975).

CHAPTER TWENTY

Glenn Gould
(1932–1982)

When not making music [Gould] became almost a different person, rather shy and embarrassed, like a young boy. (Peter Ostwald 1997)

The Canadian pianist Glenn Gould ranks as one of the outstanding modern interpreters of the keyboard music of Johann Sebastian Bach. According to Gould's biographer Peter Ostwald (1997), who knew him well, some of the eccentric behaviour he manifested late in childhood and during adolescence – a marked fear of certain physical objects, disturbances in empathy, social withdrawal, self-isolation and obsessive attention to ritualised behaviour – is suggestive of Asperger's syndrome. Since Ostwald was a professor of medicine, this opinion must carry weight. Furthermore, several psychiatrists (e.g. Fitzgerald 2005) agree with Ostwald that Gould probably had the syndrome. On the other hand Kevin Bazzana, who has written the most complete account (2004) of Gould's life, including a lengthy discussion of his personality, says that he is not persuaded.

Glenn Gould was born in Toronto on 25 September 1932. His father Russell Herbert Gold was a furrier with a prosperous business in downtown Toronto; he changed the family surname to Gould when his son was seven. His mother Flora Emma (née Greig), of Scottish ancestry, was an able musician, who taught music and sang in church. On the theory that this would have some influence, she played music to her unborn child. He was able to read music before he learned to read words, possessed absolute pitch and had a phenomenal musical memory, so that his mother compared him to Mozart.

His father described his son, an only child, as a very happy baby, with a sunny disposition and a marvellous sense of humour, but he also had a violent temper. He disliked sunlight and hated bright colours, especially red and yellow. His senses of sight, taste and smell were poor, but what he heard affected him deeply. The slightest touch could produce a quite disproportionate reaction. He avoided social contact with other children, detested group activities at school, and seemed totally unfit for any kind of sport. If someone threw a ball towards him in the school yard he would turn away petrified. A school friend recalled: 'Glenn really didn't want to work very hard. He didn't do what the teachers wanted him to do a lot of the time. His posture was terrible, as was his penmanship. All his essays and books and so on were always messy, but he was good at history, English and especially mathematics' (Ostwald 1997). Already he used to overdress on warm days. 'By the time I was six,' he used to say, 'I'd already made an important discovery: that I get along much better with animals than with humans.' He kept a variety of pets throughout his life, and could never resist rescuing stray dogs and other animals.

Another friend recalled that from childhood onwards he had a fear of germs. 'If anyone was the faintest bit sick they were not allowed to be near him. He was terrified of getting sick.' He had a lifelong dread of hospitals as repositories of germs. This hypochondria he seems to have picked up from his mother, whose admonitions he never questioned. She hated conflict and anything extreme or eccentric. 'Against impossible odds, she longed to see her son have a normal childhood, with the right amounts of fresh air and exercise and the right sort of friends' (Ostwald 1997). He was a born intellectual, she was not. He saw no reason to accept conventional opinion, however well established, while she knew no other. 'She was a woman of propriety; when she spoke it was from a tranquil world of rules and order, a world from which conflict and tension had somehow been erased' (Ostwald 1997).

As he grew older Glenn began to distance himself from his father, whose business dealings with hunters and trappers, and love of fishing, he found revolting. Later in life he would become a vegetarian and a supporter of animal welfare; in his will he specified that a sizeable part of his estate should go to the Toronto Humane Society. Glenn always sought to create an impression of fierce independence, of being someone for whom human interaction and intimacy were totally inessential. At the same time his remarkable charm, playfulness and intellect attracted people and he revelled in the attention they were willing to give him so long as he remained in control and everything went the way he wanted it to go. In this way he could make inordinate demands on his friends. When the time came, as it inevitably did, when criticism and viewpoints were expressed that he could not tolerate, he would break off the relationship abruptly. Sometime in his childhood, apparently, he had momentarily felt he was capable of inflicting serious bodily harm on his mother, even murder. The experience frightened him profoundly and he swore to himself that he would never let that inner rage reveal itself again. Bertrand Russell, we recall, also had such an experience, and the same may have been true of Jonathan Swift.

Since his father's business was flourishing, Glenn's musical education was never impeded by lack of funds. At first his mother taught him the piano until, at the age of ten, he was admitted to the Toronto Conservatory of Music, whose gold medal he was awarded after two years. By then he was already giving public recitals, but these were marred by stage fright, which became worse in later years. The best piano teacher at the conservatory, the Chilean Alberto Guerrero, took the boy under his wing. Guerrero believed that to give the hands and fingers maximum freedom the pianist's arms had to be on the same level as the keyboard. Glenn became used to sitting on a low chair and bending over the keyboard; his father had made him an adjustable chair, on which he could sit only a foot above the floor. His son used it for the rest of his life, even after the seat cushion wore out and there was nothing but the frame left to sit on.

At the same time he put the finishing touches to his distinctive piano style: the marked contrast between staccato and legato, unconventionally fast or slow tempi, exceptional rhythmic vitality, high clarity of contrapuntal texture, and deliberate emphasis on inner or hidden voices. With this style went a number of physical mannerisms that also made his performances unique. His mouth was incessantly in motion, articulating with lips or teeth the passages his fingers were executing so nimbly on the keyboard. He always hummed or sang, often loud enough to be heard even at the back of a concert hall. Sitting on his low chair, he undulated the entire upper part of his body in a circular motion consistent with the tempo he was playing, and whenever one of his hands was not busy on the keyboard, he used it like a conductor, making all sorts of expressive gestures and in effect conducting his own playing. Guerrero criticised these mannerisms but could do nothing to change them and so, after nine years, he gave up trying to teach him.

Around this time the social traits that made Gould seem eccentric also blossomed: his odd way of overdressing, his excessive use of humour and joking, and his hypersensitivity to bodily sensations that he believed to be signs of disease. Already in those days he was regularly consulting physicians and chiropractors. He was a gifted imitator of other people, their facial expressions, speech mannerisms, foreign accents and body language. Gould possessed total recall, at least for music, and so always played from memory. He usually slept most of the day, and was wide awake long into the night. He felt edgy when two other people were in the same room with him; three or more caused his social anxiety to escalate sharply. He moved with an awkward stride. In conversation words flowed out of him with unabashed vitality, making it difficult to interrupt. He liked to gossip about sex, but even those close to him doubted whether he had had any love affairs.

When he was fourteen Gould had made his concert debut with the Toronto Symphony Orchestra, in Beethoven's fourth piano concerto, after which Canada was quick to recognise his genius. As well as giving public concerts he was soon broadcasting and recording, which he preferred because no visible audience was involved and his mannerisms did not distract from the subtlety and insight of his interpretations. At first he mainly performed the classics, but later his musical repertoire began to include twentieth-century twelve-tone music. His many recordings include the complete piano music of Arnold Schoenberg and other works outside the standard piano repertoire.

Gould's fame reached its zenith in 1955, when he was twenty-three. He already had a high reputation for his performances of Bach, but it was his recording of the Goldberg Variations that made him world famous. This took place in Manhattan; it was June, but he arrived as usual in winter clothing. As well as the musical equipment he brought towels, mineral water, plenty of pills and, of course, the special chair his father made for him. Gould was in perpetual motion, conducting rhapsodically, doing a kind of dance to the music. For sustenance he munched arrowroot biscuits and drank skimmed milk. Journalists were invited to come and watch the historic recording sessions, which lasted a week. When the record was released it became a huge commercial success, even eclipsing the harpsichord version of Wanda Landowska, and he found himself in great demand around the world as a performer. Unfortunately he also developed a reputation for cancelling engagements, saying he was too ill to perform. Much of this was just hypochondria, as he was always consulting doctors about something or other. They found him a trying patient. Although he had very little understanding of how the body functioned, he liked to take charge and persuade the doctor to put him on some new drug he had heard about, usually without medical justification. He also had psychological problems and subsequently started psychoanalysis.

By this time Gould had been accepted into the inner circle of musical celebrities, not only other pianists but high-profile conductors like Bernstein and Stokowski. He yearned to become a conductor himself, but his eccentricities were too much of a drawback. His first overseas concert tour was to the Soviet Union where he introduced enthusiastic Russian audiences to works they had never heard before, due to the suppression of modern music under Stalin. His own early compositions – short pieces for piano alone and for bassoon and piano, and a long one-movement string quartet – were strongly influenced by Schoenberg.

By 1958 Gould decided to find a home of his own in Toronto; he kept changing his mind but eventually settled down in a spacious six-room penthouse apartment that remained his official base for the rest of his life. Although he used it regularly, his restless spirit often found it necessary to stay elsewhere in the city, usually in hotels. He liked to drive himself around but he frequently had minor accidents and nearly lost his licence several times. Like Béla Bartók he so disliked performing in public that in 1962 he finally abandoned the public stage, although curiously enough just before he finally did so he started a brief career as a lecturer. For radio he designed a weekly programme called *Music of Today*, in which he often took part himself. He tried his hand as a television producer, with limited success. His impersonations of old-fashioned British conductors like Adrian Boult and actors like Marlon Brando were popular, but he mainly loved to talk about himself, by this time less as pianist, more as radio producer and filmmaker.

In 1971, on the threshold of middle age, Gould had plans to record all 32 Beethoven sonatas, all 16 Handel suites and more than 50 Haydn sonatas. When his mother died, following a stroke, Gould displayed little emotion, although he experienced a profound sense of loss. She had been the recipient of all his confidences, but unfortunately she left no diary or other records that might have been useful to a biographer. He described her as a woman of tremendous faith, who sought to instil that faith in others. He strongly disapproved of his father's remarriage in 1979 to a widow and long-time friend of the family, regarding it as an insult to his mother's memory.

In his prime Gould had looked youthful and attractive physically, but now middle age, illness and unwise medication were taking their toll. His face and body had become bloated; he looked fat, flabby and stooped. His movements had become slower. His skin had acquired an unnatural pallor, due probably to lack of sunlight. He worried about his health more and more. His playing developed undesirable characteristics, for example some recordings he made of the late Beethoven piano sonatas, in which he completely rejected standard and traditional performance practices. Two days after his fiftieth birthday he suffered a stroke. His condition rapidly deteriorated and he died on 4 October 1982.

Acknowledgment

The principal sources of information in this chapter are Bazzana (2004), Fitzgerald (2005), Friedrich (1989), Ostwald (1997) and Payzant (1978).

Conclusion

It would not be difficult to add further profiles, but rather than do so it seems preferable to finish by gathering together the relevant material from the individual profiles (omitting details which do not need to be repeated) so as to provide more of an overview. To organise this conveniently I will adopt as headings the simplified version, mentioned in the Introduction, of the diagnostic criteria for Asperger's syndrome that are used before making an assessment (of course there is much more to this than just checking off points on a questionnaire). For a positive assessment the criteria should be satisfied right across development, but since we are not concerned with diagnosis here that is not so relevant. The headings, I recall, are:

- social impairments
- all-absorbing narrow interests
- repetitive routines
- speech and language peculiarities
- problems of non-verbal communication
- motor clumsiness.

The last of these is not considered essential in the case of highly intelligent people.

Social impairments

With social impairment, or more specifically *severe impairment in reciprocal social interaction*, the individual may interact poorly with peers, fail to recognise social cues, seem unable to sense the feelings of other people, and exhibit emotionally or socially inappropriate behaviour. Impairment in the domain of social interaction is the most striking feature of all forms of autism.

The problem is a reduction in empathy, or social resonance: the instinctive drive to understand another person's feelings and thoughts, and to respond to these appropriately. People with Asperger's are too preoccupied with their own private reality. Ludwig Wittgenstein, for example, had great difficulty at an emotional level: an inability to manage social relationships and communication throughout his life. He was painfully aware of his own indifference to other people and his inability to perceive of relationships with them in ways that were similar to theirs. Often he could not recognise the humanity in other human beings; as he explained, human relations were like Chinese to him. Many of those who knew him have testified to his egocentricity and lack of awareness of the presence of other people and their feelings: he imposed a confrontation in all his relationships. 'Although I cannot give affection I have a great need for it,' he wrote.

People who display scrupulous honesty and frankness, with little or no tact, may seem innocent and sincere, but also tactless and rude. Wittgenstein, again, was feared because of his shocking frankness. Patricia Highsmith never realised when she had hurt other people; she was incapable of not saying whatever was in her mind. Béla Bartók saw no point in the polite urbanities of social intercourse. Alfred Kinsey had no small talk, nor did Wittgenstein.

Although individuals with Asperger's have a strong desire to be popular and liked, to be part of society, and to be accepted by those around them, they find difficulty in maintaining friendships. Friends tend to be dropped suddenly and totally, with an all-or-nothing ruthlessness. Simone Weil, for example, chose her friends imperiously, but when she saw an unfavourable trait in one of them, she was capable of abruptly ending a relationship with a horizontal cutting gesture of her hand. Bertrand Russell was unable to maintain any sort of reciprocal relationship with relatives and friends, who felt he was almost devoid of normal warmth and emotions.

Individuals with Asperger's usually find ways to manage social relationships by the time they grow up, but these are not the normal ways. Excessive politeness and formality is one such strategy. Jonathan Swift 'contrived to dominate any conversation with a blaze of politeness'. John Howard was 'very polite'. 'I never met anyone so polite as [Eric] Satie,' said Madeleine Milhaud. The manners of Russell were 'formal, courteous and old-fashioned'. Bartók was 'reservedly polite' and Kinsey 'charmingly courteous'. Another common strategy is cracking jokes. One of Satie's friends said: 'I doubt whether he ever stopped being witty, precise, a joker.' In India, at least, Ramanujan was described as friendly and gregarious, always full of fun; even on his deathbed he cracked jokes. Although Glenn Gould's remarkable charm, playfulness and intellect attracted people, his constant wise-cracking was found tiresome.

Individuals with Asperger's are unable to tell if someone they are speaking to is getting bored. They tend to talk *at* other people, rather than *to* them, telling more than they want to know about topics of interest only to themselves. Thus Ramanujan would open his note-books and explain intricate theorems and formulae without least suspecting that they were beyond the understanding or knowledge of his listener. Kinsey 'peppered people with facts'; people who came to view his collection of erotica were given an interminable lecture. When replying to a question Alan Turing was liable to go on talking for hours, while 'words flowed out of Gould with unabashed vitality, making it difficult to interrupt'.

Let us run through the profiles looking for signs of the impairment of social interaction. Michelangelo Buonarroti said he had no friends of any sort, and wanted none. Philip of Spain never exuded warmth; from an early age he became adept at concealing his feelings and constraining his emotions. Being alone was said to be his greatest pleasure. Isaac Newton, we are told, was singularly unable to make friendships; he did little to encourage others to like him. Swift, a man of irresistible charm in personal intercourse, was also a man of intense responses, turning to towering rage, and 'when he was angry, his natural severity becomes frightening, it is scarcely possible to imagine looks, or features, that carried with them more terror and austerity'. Vanessa complained of his 'killing words' and the 'awful look which struck her dumb'.

Henry Cavendish, by contrast, had a pathologically shy and nervous disposition: he was described as the coldest and most indifferent of mortals, who mainly lived as a recluse owing to a morbid dislike of society. Thomas Jefferson was inordinately shy as a youth; later he was still said to be 'reserved towards the world at large'. People who knew Vincent van Gogh as a child recalled that he had no social life but would wander off on his own, silent and morose. Relatives, schoolmates, teachers and acquaintances described his curious aloofness; not only were his brothers and sisters strangers to him, one said, he was a stranger to himself. A friend of Satie's said: 'I doubt whether anybody was entrusted with the favour of a heartfelt outburst from him... I doubt whether anyone found warmth in Satie's company.' Throughout his life Russell felt an acute sense of isolation and loneliness. His relationship with each of his first three wives appears to have been ruined by exploitation, cruelty and viciousness, and by a lack of love and understanding.

Albert Einstein was described as shy, lonely and withdrawn from the world, as a child, unsociable and 'adrift forever in his foolish dreams'. Very early he set himself the task of establishing himself as an entirely separate entity, influenced as little as possible by other people. 'I'm not much with people,' he used to say. His elusive coldness towards colleagues was well known. He was little attached to those around him and had no desire to be involved emotionally in the society in which he lived. As one of his biographers remarked, 'He never really needed human contacts; he deliberately freed himself more and more from all emotional dependence in order to become entirely self-sufficient.'

As a child, Bartók found it difficult to form friendships with other children, while as an adult we are told that he was 'almost painfully shy' and 'incurably nervous'. One observer thought he had built an invisible barrier of defence between himself and the outside world. Few felt really comfortable in his presence. Kinsey, as a boy, made no close friends; he was always reading, not socialising. At Indiana University he made few friends, virtually none with older colleagues. He was ill-at-ease in the company of others, and his extraordinary intensity made many people feel the same in his presence. Turing remarked: 'I have more contact with this bed than with other people.' Weil displayed a terrible preoccupation with herself, refusing to make any concessions to the requirements and conventions of social life. Highsmith, like Ramanujan, was not aware of any nuances of conversation. Although Andy Warhol had an active social life, he practised detachment from emotions and people. At parties he would sit in a corner and say nothing. 'He had no consideration for other people,' we are told. 'He lacked all amenities, was socially inept and showed little or no appreciation for anything.' As a child Gould avoided social contact with other children and detested group activities at school. In later years he felt edgy when two other people were in the same room with him; three or more caused his social anxiety to escalate sharply.

All-absorbing narrow interests

With *the presence of one or more all-absorbing narrow interest patterns,* the individual has a narrow but intense focus that leaves little time for other activities. There is a repetitive quality to the specific interest or interest patterns.

Michelangelo was obsessed with art. For Philip of Spain his fascination with building operations would be a good example of an all-absorbing narrow interest. In the case of Newton we can cite his obsessive interest in alchemy, his fascination with biblical chronology, and his youthful feelings of guilt. Swift wrote to Stella almost every day: his letter-writing habits could clearly be seen as obsessive behaviour, likewise his determination to take regular exercise. Dinner guests of Cavendish were advised that it was useless to try to engage him in conversation on any non-scientific topic. Jefferson kept detailed records of his personal expenditure throughout his life, and was obsessively concerned with the organisation of the University of Virginia and the planning of his residence at Monticello.

Van Gogh had an obsession first with religion, then with painting. Satie had various obsessions, such as the precise way his suitcase was packed. Russell was fascinated by trains and timetables, according to one of his daughters. His passionate quest for mathematical perfection could also be seen as an obsession. Ramanujan was 'ensnared by pure mathematics, he lost interest in everything else'. In relation to mathematics he had an 'intellectual passion and fierce unbending intensity that would rule the rest of his life'. 'He was all maths, he could not get enough of it.' Wittgenstein focused exclusively on one area of philosophy to the exclusion of all other areas and all other activities. He felt that nothing was worth doing except producing great philosophical works. He was given to being lost in thought and resented being interrupted. The young Warhol 'never had much to say and it was always about his work. He was really wrapped up in his work.'

Repetitive routines

With repetitive routines, or more specifically *the imposition of routines, rituals and interests on self or others,* individuals with Asperger's exhibit a great variety of fixations, obsessions and compulsions, but those we have noticed in the profiles are among the most common. They are easily upset when their expectations are not met or their routines are disturbed.

The administrative routine of Philip of Spain was highly repetitive, as was the way he went round the royal residences. Newton had a compulsion to make draft after draft of many of his papers, for example as many as eighteen, only differing slightly from each other, for the first chapter of his book on biblical chronology, and he even felt a need to copy routine documents relating to the business at the Mint. We may add the meticulous records he kept of his experiments. Swift and Jefferson were very fond of making lists, and kept detailed accounts of everything they spent. Howard, we are told, 'was a lover of regularity in all his affairs and was particularly noted for strict punctuality and for the exact and methodical disposition of time'. Cavendish displayed a clockwork regularity in all his transactions with life. Satie also had a fixed daily routine. Russell was 'terribly punctual', and liked everything to be in its place. Bartók's passion for collecting folk songs extended to specimens of traditional handicrafts that he liked to arrange in a particular way. Ramanujan as a child would line up the household utensils systematically from one wall to the other.

Wittgenstein spent a great deal of his time arranging and rearranging his philosophical works and transferring them from one copybook to another. He would listen to the same piece of music over and over again. He declared that it did not matter to him what he ate, so long as it was always the same. At the Bevans, 'He was very demanding and exacting although his tastes were very simple. It was understood that his bath would be ready, his meals on time and that the events of the day would run to a regular pattern.' Swift was preoccupied with cleanliness, and its opposite, filth, especially when it came to women. Kinsey too had an obsession with personal hygiene, as did Philip of Spain. Highsmith had a fixation about house cleaning and took several showers a day. Also, 'if you moved an ashtray in one of her houses, she would immediately put it back in the same place'. Warhol said he lived off Campbell's soup for twenty years of his early life. Later he had a compulsive need to collect things and to check that nothing was missing. Gould loved making lists, throughout his life.

Individuals with Asperger's tend to be careless of their appearance and to dress in the same way, regardless of the occasion. Michelangelo, for example, changed his clothing so rarely that his clothes stuck to his skin. Newton was said to be slovenly and untidy in his dress, wore down-at-heel shoes and hair scarcely combed. The frugal Swift always wore his clerical gown, saying such gowns were cheaper than fashionable coats. Cavendish retained the style of dress of his youth for the rest of his life. Jefferson preferred an informal mode of dress; as chief executive he greeted dignitaries in odd frayed clothing, worn-out bedroom slippers and with uncombed hair. Van Gogh took no interest in his personal appearance. Satie, in his 'velvet gentleman' persona, dressed in one of a dozen identical suits. Although Einstein kept a wardrobe of seven identical suits to wear on formal occasions, his ordinary dress was casual; he favoured sweatshirts, leather jackets and sandals. Bartók was attached to a threadbare brown overcoat. Wittgenstein always dressed in the same way, never wearing a tie or hat. Turing cared little for his personal appearance. Weil wore a drab unisex outfit. Warhol dressed like a street urchin up to the age of thirty. Even in the warmest weather Gould overdressed in overcoat, sweater, beret, muffler and gloves; at public performances he would wear a crumpled business suit with unmatched socks and untied shoelaces.

Speech and language peculiarities

With peculiarities of speech and language, the individual may use stilted or pedantic language or odd prosody, in speech or writing. There may be peculiar voice characteristics: the individual may speak at times in a strangely swallowed tone of voice, may stammer when nervous or have trouble starting conversations. There may be impairment of comprehension, for example a tendency to interpret statements literally, a failure to recognise or understand irony, trouble with words having multiple meanings, and a lack of artifice. The individual may talk too much or too little, may speak too rapidly or in an unregulated tone, ignoring the need to adjust speech according to the understanding of others.

Philip of Spain was often tongue-tied, and when he spoke it was in such a low voice that even those very close to him could hardly hear what he said. When Newton was in the company of others he contributed little to the conversation. Howard's voice verged on the effeminate; he was unable to speak or write with grammatical correctness. 'He was rather pragmatical in his speech, very polite, but expressing himself in a manner that seemed to belong to two hundred years ago.' Cavendish was very taciturn; his voice was hesitant and somewhat shrill: he uttered shrill cries as he moved about. Jefferson stammered; when he tried to raise his voice in volume it fell in pitch and he became inarticulate. Van Gogh spoke with a deep and melancholic voice, his language was said to be queer and awkward, his speech halting. Satie spoke very softly, hardly opening his mouth, but he delivered each word in an inimitable, precise way. Einstein was a late talker; he was still not considered fluent in speech at the age of seven. Also he was echolalic. Bartók was over two years old before he began to talk; when he did so he spoke complete sentences right away. The intonation of his speaking voice was 'exceedingly grey and monotonous'. He rarely emphasised a particular word; his words flowed out completely evenly. His voice was also said to be 'excessively deep, disciplined and serene', his speech 'unusually clear, plain and at the same time, restrained, matter-of-fact and concentrated'. Ramanujan hardly spoke a word until the age of three. Russell had an almost affectedly clear enunciation of words and preciseness of expression. Wittgenstein did not start speaking until he was four; he stammered in his youth. As an adult he 'always spoke emphatically and with a distinctive intonation…his voice was resonant, the pitch being somewhat higher than that of the normal male voice. His words came out, not fluently but with great force.' Turing's speech was hesitant and high-pitched; he had a shrill stammer and a braying laugh. Weil's voice was high-pitched and monotonous. Warhol talked in a breathless whisper until he changed the way he spoke, mumbling monosyllabic, often incoherent, replies to questions. He tended to repeat single words over and over again. As Peter York said: 'The absolute flatness [of his voice], the affectlessness, meant that you couldn't see behind it at all.'

We are told that Newton would with great acuteness answer a question, but would never start one. He would sometimes be silent and thoughtful for above a quarter of an hour together, and all the while almost as if he was saying his prayers, but that when he did speak it was very much to the purpose. Einstein was a confusing lecturer, giving specific examples followed by seemingly unrelated general principles. Occasionally he would lose his train of thought while writing on the blackboard; a few minutes later he would emerge as from a trance and go on to something different. He would sometimes fall silent in the course of conversation, rise to his feet without a word, or remain sitting motionless: he would be unreachable. Wittgenstein was given to being lost in thought and disliked being interrupted. In his writing he made no effort to help the reader to understand, while in teaching he just spoke his thoughts aloud, largely in monologue.

Individuals with Asperger's tend to have a strange sense of humour, or apparently none at all. Philip of Spain was never known to laugh. Humphrey could only remember Newton laughing once in five years, and that was when someone asked what geometry was good for, 'upon which Sir Isaac was very merry'. 'He used a good many sayings, bordering on joke or wit; in company he was easily made to smile if not to laugh.' Swift seldom if ever laughed. At Cardington, Howard would:

> arrive every morning, never missing a single day, under the buttress of the garden wall, just as the bread-cart was passing at its punctual hour; when he would purchase a loaf, throw it into the garden, and then entering at the gate, would cry out laughingly [to the gardener] 'Harry! See if there is not something for your family there among the cabbages.' (Aikin 1792)

Jefferson was only occasionally known to smile. Satie seldom if ever laughed normally, but he was sometimes seized by unexpected bursts of laughter, which he would stifle with one hand. Ramanujan's jokes were said to be primitive. Einstein had a ribald sense of humour and a loud guffaw. Bartók rarely laughed; his sense of humour was 'not very developed'. Warhol hardly ever laughed. Wittgenstein's sense of humour was said to be childish, with an element of crudeness. Highsmith had a raucous, earthy and quite unsophisticated sense of humour. Turing had a braying laugh. Gould had an uproarious sense of humour and a cackling laugh.

Problems of non-verbal communication

With such problems, the individual uses awkward body language, sits in an awkward way, rocks in a seated position or flaps hands when nervous or distressed, wears an unexpressive face or faraway look, and has a peculiar stiff gaze. The tone of voice can be peculiar, with unusual emphasis on certain words. Since so much of communication is non-verbal, this is no less important than verbal communication.

Individuals with Asperger's often have difficulty with initiating and maintaining eye contact, particularly with strangers. However, the gaze may instead be stiff, strange, peculiar or abnormally intense, as can often be seen in photographs and other portraits. The gaze of Philip of Spain was so penetrating as to be quite disconcerting. Newton showed limited facial expression, but had a lively and piercing eye. Swift had 'a natural severity of face'. Howard's gaze was said to be penetrating. Jefferson had a clear and penetrating eye. Van Gogh had an eagle eye. Russell also had a peculiar stiff gaze. Einstein found it difficult to make eye contact. Ramanujan had a peculiar stiff gaze and shining eye. Bartók rarely made eye contact with other people, but when he did so his gaze was said to be penetrating. Wittgenstein had a peculiar stiff gaze; his eyes were deep and often fierce in expression. Weil had a piercing gaze; the eagerness in her eyes was said to be almost unbearable. Turing usually avoided eye contact, but photographs show a peculiar stiff gaze. Gould was reluctant to look people in the eye more than glancingly. It has been suggested that such people use peripheral vision when other people use central vision, and that these different types of vision are processed differently in the brain.

Motor clumsiness

The last criterion is motor clumsiness, although there is some disagreement among the experts as to whether or not this should be a diagnostic requirement in the case of highly intelligent individuals. There was something peculiar about the gait of Philip of Spain. Cavendish had a quick and uneasy gait; he walked leaning forward on his toes. There was an air of stiffness in Jefferson's manner, we are told: he failed to swing his arms normally when walking, and made awkward gestures when speaking. Ramanujan was unable to tie a necktie; like Cavendish, he walked leaning forward on his toes. Van Gogh's gestures were described as lively and his movements jerky. Bartók's movements often seemed to be 'hesitating and somewhat stiff'; his acknowledgement of applause, after a recital, was awkward and graceless. Wittgenstein had a peculiar gait and unusual gestures. Einstein found it hard to tie his shoelaces. Kinsey was said to be maladroit. Weil was notoriously clumsy; she walked with long jerky steps. There was gaucherie and lack of grace in Highsmith's movements. Gould had a teenager's slouch and a hunched, loping splay-footed gait.

Difficulty with the physical act of writing is common among people with Asperger's. Philip of Spain had a strange loopy hand, difficult to decipher. Newton had tiny handwriting. A teacher said Turing's handwriting was the worst he had ever seen. Bartók wrote in a small, clear script. Satie also wrote with extraordinary precision, and Wittgenstein was dyslexic, probably so was Einstein. Weil wrote sloppily and slowly, while Gould's handwriting was said to be terrible, despite the perfection of his musical performances.

Of course, the diagnostic markers do not exhaust all the distinguishing features of Asperger's syndrome. There are so many different idiosyncrasies and just what they are may have nothing to do with the syndrome. Several of my subjects exhibited remarkable powers of memory. Michelangelo, for example, had an extraordinary visual memory. When a former school friend asked Kinsey about the field trips they used to take together, he replied: 'I can recall every single spot, I think, and each object we found on those trips.' Warhol had an 'elephantine' memory. Gould possessed total recall, at least for music.

People with Asperger's are often hypersensitive to certain types of sensation. Perhaps Swift is suggesting this when he wrote that:

> as soon as I [Gulliver] entered the house, my wife took me in her arms and kissed me; at which, having not been used to the touch of that odious animal for so many years, I fell in a swoon of almost an hour... I could not endure my wife or children in my presence, the very smell of them was intolerable. (Swift 1933)

Jefferson required soft clothing on certain parts of his body but tight clothing across his chest. Einstein cut the sleeves off his shirts. Warhol had a great talent for avoiding personal contact and felt it necessary to use a particular kind of underwear. Swift and Gould displayed a revulsion to most forms of physical contact, experiencing it as not merely unpleasant but highly threatening. Weil was also averse to physical contact, although she played rugby football. At school Ramanujan refused to play team games. In the supermarket Highsmith was overwhelmed by sensory stimulation; there were too many people and too much noise and she just could not handle it. Undue sensitivity to sounds, smells and touch are very typical of people with Asperger's.

Individuals with Asperger's may interact socially very well with people who are not their peers. Among the subjects of my profiles, Satie, Einstein, Bartók and Kinsey seem to have felt a special empathy with children. In her book *Thinking in Pictures* (1996), Temple Grandin describes the unusual understanding she has of the feelings of animals, which approach her with confidence.

Bartók also had this empathy with animals, and also with peasants, whose lives were likewise rooted in the land. Gould was also an animal lover, while Wittgenstein was greatly attached to birds. Highsmith adored cats, which are affectionate without being too demonstrative. People with Asperger's often develop an impersonal kind of benevolence and support good causes, for example penal reform in the case of Howard, the improvement of mankind in the case of Jefferson, world peace in the case of Einstein, the French working class in the case of Weil, and animal welfare in the case of Gould. Another peculiarity, which has been noted by Gillberg (2002), is that they tend to look young for their ages; we saw this with Bartók, Turing and Gould.

Intimate relationships are very difficult for people with Asperger's to maintain. Some of my subjects, of either sex, retained an unusually close relationship with their mothers long after they became adults. That was true of Bartók, Ramanujan, Weil, Highsmith, Warhol and Gould, for example. Swift said he had never seen a woman for whose sake he would part with the middle of his bed. Cavendish was a mysogynist. Russell seems to have mistaken lust for love and used his various partners to fulfil his sexual needs and desires. One of them said that he was cold to women, selfish and goat-like; another spoke of his terrific sexual urge which caused him to assume the repulsive expression of a lustful satyr. Wittgenstein said of himself that he was unable to give affection. Gould told a friend that his basic problem with women was that he would not accept love; any expression of affection would cause him to panic. Several of my subjects had homosexual tendencies, for example Michelangelo, Kinsey, Wittgenstein, Turing, Highsmith and Warhol.

Most of my subjects remained single. Of the others, Jefferson did marry. Einstein married twice, although neither marriage could be described as particularly successful. He was physically attractive to women, in his youth, and had a number of affairs. Howard and Bartók also married twice, Philip of Spain four times. Russell was a womaniser who also married four times. All the marriages, except Philip's second, Howard's first, Russell's first and last, and Einstein's second, resulted in children; the spouses did not have Asperger's themselves. Most of my Asperger possibles could be violent, certainly Swift, van Gogh, Satie, Russell and Einstein, and where there were spouses the violence might be directed towards them.

Like many other individuals with Asperger's, Cavendish was interested in music, the art that speaks most directly to the feelings. Jefferson liked to sing or hum music to himself while he was thinking. Einstein had a passion for music, as a way of experiencing and expressing emotion that is impersonal. He is reported to have said that music was as important to him as physics: 'it is a way for me to be independent of people'; on another occasion he described it as the most important thing in his life. Wittgenstein could whistle long pieces of music with great accuracy and expression. Like many others with Asperger's he had perfect pitch. He said that music was so important to him that he could hardly put into words its enormous importance. At one time he had ambitions to become a conductor. Bartók became quite a different person when he started to play the piano, and perhaps the same might be said of Gould. It has been found that some autistic people lose all signs of the disorder when music is played, although the signs return as soon as the music stops.

Individuals with Asperger's syndrome have strong emotions themselves but seem immune to the emotional forces that bind people together. Maintaining control is the only way that they can survive in a complex world full of mixed emotions and inconsistent feelings, all of which are a complete mystery to them. For Michelangelo loss of control could cause great frustration. 'Newton's aim was to make me come under him,' said Flamsteed, 'and force me to comply with his humours.' 'Nobody could be a warmer friend,' it was said of Swift, 'but it was on condition that his friends should be part of himself. He annexed other persons rather than attracted them. He was adamant that no one should ever have power over him: the power to melt his self-possession, the power to hurt.' Wittgenstein said that he could only handle relationships on his own terms and where he had total control. There was also something in Kinsey's personality that made him want to dominate other people. Gould revelled in the attention of others so long as he remained in control and everything went the way he wanted it to go. The need to retain control is vital to people with Asperger's, and underlies various other behaviour patterns, such as their need to establish rules and inflexible routines. However, a discussion of the reasons behind the way people with Asperger's behave lies outside the scope of this book.

Bibliography

Acworth, B. (1947) *Swift*. London: Eyre & Spottiswoode.

Aikin, J. (1792) *A View of the Character and Public Services of the Late John Howard*. London: J. Johnson.

Arshad, M. and Fitzgerald, M. (2004) 'Did Michelangelo (1475–1564) have high-functioning autism?' *Journal of Medical Biography 12*, 115–120.

Asperger, H. (1944) 'Die "autischen Psychopathen" im Kindesalter.' *Archiv für Psychiatrie und Nervenkrankheiten 117*, 76–136.

Baron-Cohen, S. (2001) *Understanding Other Minds*. Oxford: Oxford University Press.

Baron-Cohen, S. (2003) *The Essential Difference: Men, Women and the Extreme Male Brain*. London: Allen Lane.

Bazzana, K. (2004) *Wondrous Strange: The Life and Work of Glenn Gould*. New Haven, CT: Yale University Press.

Beck, J. (1975) *Michelangelo: A Lesson in Anatomy*. London: Phaidon Press.

Berman, F., Fitzgerald, M. and Hayes, J. (eds) (1996) *The Danger of Words and Writings on Wittgenstein*. Bristol: Thoemmes Press.

Berry, A.J. (1960) *Henry Cavendish: His Life and Scientific Work*. London: Hutchinson & Co.

Bockris, V. (1989) *Warhol*. London: Muller.

Bondeson, L. and Bondeson, A.G. (2003) 'Michelangelo's divine goitre.' *Journal of the Royal Society of Medicine 96*, 609–611.

Bourdon, D. (1989) *Warhol*. New York: Harry N. Abrahams.

Brian, D. (1996) *Einstein: A Life*. New York: John Wiley & Sons.

Brink, A. (1989) *Bertrand Russell: The Psychobiography of a Moralist*. New Jersey: Humanities Press International.

Brougham, Lord H. (1872) *Lives of Philosophers of the Time of George III*. Edinburgh: Adam and Charles Black.

Brown, J.B. (1823) *The Life of John Howard*. London: Thomas and George Underwood.

Challis, N. and Dewey, H.W. (1974) 'The blessed fools of Old Russia.' *Jahrbucher fur Geschichte Osteuropas, NS 22*, 1–11.

Chalmers, K. (1995) *Béla Bartók*. London: Phaidon.

Condivi, A. (1976) *The Life of Michelangelo* (trans. A.S. Wohl and ed. H. Wohl). Oxford: Phaidon Press.

Cooke, A.Z. (1999) 'Andy and autism.' *Art News 5*.

De Morgan, A. (1885) *Newton: His Friend and His Niece*. London.

Dinnage, R. (2004) *Alone! Alone! Lives of Some Outsider Women*. New York: New York Review of Books.

du Plessix Gray, F. (2001) *Simone Weil*. London: Weidenfeld & Nicolson.

Ehrenpreis, I. (1958) *The Personality of Jonathan Swift*. London: Methuen.

Ellis, J.J. (1997) *American Sphinx*. New York: Alfred A. Knopf.

Engelmann, P. (1967) *Letters from Ludwig Wittgenstein with a Memoir* (trans. I. Furtmuller). Oxford: Basil Blackwell.

Erpel, F. (1965) *Van Gogh Self-portraits*. Oxford: Bruno Cassiror.

Fara, H. (2002) *Newton: The Making of a Genius*. London: Macmillan.

Field, J. (1850) *The Life of John Howard*. London: Longmans.

Fitzgerald, M. (1999a) 'Did Isaac Newton have Asperger's Syndrome?' *European Child and Adolescent Psychiatry Journal 8*, 204.

Fitzgerald, M. (1999b) 'Alfred Kinsey's Asperger disorder.' *Journal of Autism and Developmental Disorders 29*, 346–347.

Fitzgerald, M. (2000) 'Einstein: brain and behaviour.' *Journal of Autism and Developmental Disorders 29*, 620–621.

Fitzgerald, M. (2001) 'Was Spinoza autistic?' *Philosophers' Magazine*, Spring, 15–16.

Fitzgerald, M. (2002) 'Did "Stonewall" Jackson have Asperger's syndrome?' *Irish Psychiatrist 3*, 223–224.

Fitzgerald, M. (2004) *Autism and Creativity*. Hove and New York: Brunner-Routledge.

Fitzgerald, M. (2005) *The Genesis of Artistic Creativity*. London: Jessica Kingsley Publishers.

Fitzgerald, M. and Lyons, V. (2003) 'Did Bertrand Russell suffer from a neurodevelopmental disorder?' *Irish Psychiatrist 4*, 171–178.

Fölsing, A. (1997) *Albert Einstein: A Biography*. New York: Viking.

Forster, J. (1875) *The Life of Jonathan Swift*. London: John Murray.

French, A.P. (ed.) (1979) *Einstein: A Centenary Volume*. London: Heinemann.

Friedrich, O. (1989) *Glenn Gould: A Life and Variations*. London: Lime Tree.

Frith, U. (ed.) (1991) *Autism and Asperger Syndrome*. Cambridge: Cambridge University Press.

Frith, U. (2003) *Autism: Explaining the Enigma*. Oxford: Basil Blackwell.

Gaythorne-Hardy, J. (1998) *Sex – The Measure of All Things – A Life of Alfred C. Kinsey*. London: Chatto & Windus.

Gillberg, C. (1992) 'Savant-syndrome'. In R. Vejlsgaard (ed.) *Medicinsk Arsbok*. Copenhagen: Munsgaard.

Gillberg, C. (2002) *A Guide to Asperger Syndrome*. Cambridge: Cambridge University Press.

Gillies, M. (1990) *Bartók Remembered*. London: Faber & Faber.

Gillmor, A. (1988) *Erik Satie*. Basingstoke: Macmillan.

Gleick, J. (2003) *Isaac Newton*. London: Pantheon.

Glendinning, V. (1988) *Jonathan Swift*. London: Hutchinson.

Grandin, T. (1988) 'Teaching tips from a recovered autistic.' *Focus on Autistic Behaviour 3*, 1–8.

Grandin, T. (1992) 'An Insider View of Autism.' In E. Schopler and G.B. Mesibov (eds) *High-Functioning Individuals with Autism*. New York: Plenum Press.

Grandin, T. (1996) *Thinking in Pictures*. New York: Vintage Books.

Hackett, P. (ed.) (1989) *The Andy Warhol Diaries*. London: Simon & Schuster.

Haddon, M. (2003) *The Curious Incident of the Dog in the Night-time*. London: Jonathan Cape.

Harding, J. (1975) *Erik Satie*. London: Secker & Warburg.

Herschman, D.J. and Lieb, J. (1998) *Manic Depression and Creativity.* Buffalo, NY:
   Prometheus.
Highfield, R. and Carter, P. (1993) *The Private Lives of Albert Einstein.* London: Faber &
   Faber.
Hodges, A. (1983) *Alan Turing: The Enigma.* London: Burnett Books.
Hoffmann, B. with H. Dukas (1972) *Albert Einstein: Creator and Rebel.* New York: Viking.
Hoopmann, K. (2003) *Haze.* London: Jessica Kingsley Publishers.
James, I. (2002) *Remarkable Mathematicians.* Cambridge: Cambridge University Press and
   Washington, DC: Mathematical Association of America.
James, I. (2003a) *Remarkable Physicists.* Cambridge: Cambridge University Press.
James, I. [with commentary by Simon Baron-Cohen] (2003b) 'Singular scientists.' *Journal
   of the Royal Society of Medicine 96*, 36–39.
Jamison, K.R. (1993) *Touched with Fire.* New York: Simon & Schuster.
Jones, J.H. (1997) *Alfred C. Kinsey: A Public/Private Life.* New York: W.W. Norton.
Jungnickel, C. and McCormmack, R. (1999) *Cavendish: The Experimental Life.*
   Philadelphia, PA: American Philosophical Society.
Kamen, H. (1997) *Philip of Spain.* New Haven, CT, and London: Yale University Press.
Kanigel, R. (1991) *The Man who Knew Infinity: A Life of the Genius Ramanujan.* London:
   Scribners.
Kanner, L. (1943) 'Autistic disturbances of affective contact.' *Nervous Child 2*, 217–250.
Keynes, M. (1995) 'The personality of Isaac Newton.' *Notes and Records of the Royal Society
   of London 49*, 1–56.
Kreisel, G. (1973) 'Bertrand Arthur William Russell, Earl Russell.' *Biographical Memoirs of
   the Royal Society of London 19*, 583–620.
Ledgin, N. (2000) *Diagnosing Jefferson: Evidence of a Condition that Guided his Beliefs,
   Behaviour and Personal Associations.* Arlington, TX: Future Horizons.
Ledgin, N. (2002) *Asperger's and Self-Esteem: Insight and Hope through Role Models.* Arlington,
   TX: Future Horizons.
Liebert, R. (1983) *Michelangelo: A Psychoanalytic Study of His Life and Images.* New Haven,
   CT: Yale University Press.
Lubin, A.J. (1975) *Stranger on the Earth: The Life of Vincent van Gogh.* St Alban's: Paladin.
Lucas, P. (2001) 'John Howard and Asperger's Syndrome: psychopathology and
   philanthropy.' *History of Psychiatry 12*, 73–101.
Malcolm, N. (1984) *Ludwig Wittgenstein: A Memoir with a Biographical Sketch by GH von
   Wright (2nd edition with Wittgenstein's letters to Malcolm).* Oxford: Oxford University
   Press.
Manuel, F.E. (1963) *Isaac Newton: Historian.* Cambridge: Cambridge University Press.
McGuiness, B. (1988) *Wittgenstein: A Life.* London: Duckworth.
Monk, R. (1990) *Ludwig Wittgenstein: The Duty of Genius.* London: Jonathan Cape.
Monk, R. (1996) *Bertrand Russell: The Spirit of Solitude 1872–1920.* London: Jonathan
   Cape.
Monk, R. (2000) *Bertrand Russell: The Ghost of Madness 1921–1970.* London: Jonathan
   Cape.
Mooregate, C. (1992) *Bertrand Russell.* London: Sinclair Stevenson.
More, L.T. (1934) *Isaac Newton – A Biography.* New York: Charles Scribner's Sons.
Mulcahy, R. (2004) *Philip II of Spain: Patron of the Arts.* Dublin: Four Courts Press.

Nabokov,V. (1994) *The Luzhin Defence* (trans. M. Scammell). London: Penguin.

Newman, M.H.A. (1955) 'Alan Mathison Turing.' *Biographical Memoirs of the Royal Society* *10,* 253–263.

O'Connell, H. and Fitzgerald, M. (2003) 'Did Alan Turing have Asperger's syndrome?' *Irish Journal of Psychological Medicine 20,* 28–31.

Oliveros de Castro, M.T. and Subiza Martin, E. (1956) *Felipe II: Studio Medico-Historico.* Madrid: Aguilar.

Orledge, R. (1995) *Satie Remembered* (trans. R. Nichols). London and Boston, MA: Faber & Faber.

Ostwald, P. (1997) *Glenn Gould: The Ecstasy and Tragedy of a Genius.* New York and London: W.W. Norton.

Overbye, D. (2003) *Einstein in Love: A Scientific Romance.* New York: Viking.

Pais, A. (1982) *Subtle is the Lord – The Science and Life of Albert Einstein.* Oxford: Clarendon Press.

Parker, G. (1979) *Philip II.* London: Hutchinson.

Parker, G. (1998) *The Grand Strategy of Philip II.* New Haven, CT: Yale University Press.

Payzant, G. (1978) *Glenn Gould, Music and Mind.* Toronto: Van Nostrand, Reinhold.

Pennanen, M.F. (1995) 'Vincent van Gogh: what do his letters suggest about his diagnosis?' *Journal of Medical Biography 3,* 43–49.

Petrement, S. (1976) *Simone Weil: A Life* (trans. R. Rosenthal). New York: Pantheon.

Ratey, J. and Johnson, C. (1997) *Shadow Syndromes.* New York: Pantheon.

Rewald, J. (1956, 1962) *Post-Impressionism: From Van Gogh to Gauguin.* New York: The Museum of Modern Art.

Russell, B. (1967, 1968, 1969) *The Autobiography of Bertrand Russell. 1872–1914,* 1914–1944, 1944–1968. London: Atlantic Monthly Press.

Sacks, O. (1995) *An Anthropologist on Mars.* London: Picador (Macmillan).

Sacks, O. (2001a) *Uncle Tungsten.* London: Picador Books.

Sacks, O. (2001b) 'Henry Cavendish: an early case of Asperger's syndrome?' *Neurology* *57,* 1347.

Schott, R. (1983) *Michelangelo.* London: Thames and Hudson.

Southward, M. (1958) *John Howard Prison Reformer: An Account of His Life and Travels.* London: Independent Press.

Sowell, T. (2001) *The Einstein Syndrome.* New York: Basic Books.

Ssucharewa, G.E. (1926) 'Die schizoiden Psychopathien im Kindesalter.' *Monatsschrift für Psychiatrie und Neurologie 60,* 235–261.

Stevens, H. (1993) *The Life and Music of Béla Bartók* (prep. by M. Gillies). Oxford: Clarendon Press.

Storr, A. (1972) *The Dynamics of Creation.* London: Martin Secker & Warburg.

Storr, A. (1985) 'Isaac Newton.' *British Medical Journal 291,* 1779–1784.

Storr, A. (1988) *The School of Genius.* London: André Deutsch.

Stukeley, W. (1936) *Memoirs of Sir Isaac Newton's Life* (ed. A. Hastings White). London: Taylor & Francis.

Swift, J. (1933) *Gulliver's Travels.* Oxford: Oxford University Press.

Szatmari, P., Brenner, P. and Nagy, J. (1989) 'Asperger's Syndrome: a review of clinical features.' *Canadian Journal of Psychiatry 34,* 544–560.

Times Literary Supplement (2000) 5 December, p.3.

Trilling, L. (1948) 'Sex and science: the Kinsey report.' *Partisan Review*, April, 460–476.

Turing, S. (1959) *Alan M. Turing*. Cambridge: Heffers.

Vallentin, A. (1954) *Einstein*. London: Weidenfeld & Nicholson.

van Gogh, V. (1988) *The Complete Letters of Vincent van Gogh*. Boston, MA: Little Brown & Co.

Warhol, A. (1975) *The Philosophy of Andy Warhol (From A to B and Back Again)*. San Diego, CA: Harcourt Brace.

Webb, B. (1948) *Our Partnership*. London: Longmans Green.

Weil, S. (1952) *The Need for Roots*. New York: G.P. Putnam's Sons

Wertheimer, M. (1959) *Productive Thinking*. New York: Harper & Row.

Westfall, R.S. (1993) *The Life of Isaac Newton*. Cambridge: Cambridge University Press.

White, M. (1997) *Isaac Newton: The Last Sorcerer*. London: Fourth Estate.

Wilson, A. (2003) *Beautiful Shadow: A Life of Patricia Highsmith*. London: Bloomsbury Publishing.

Wilson, G. (1851) *The Life of the Honourable Henry Cavendish*. London: Cavendish Society.

Wing, L. (2001) *The Autistic Spectrum*. London: Constable.

Wolff, S. (1995) *Loners*. London: Routledge.

Wood, A. (1987) *Bertrand Russell: The Passionate Sceptic*. London: Allen and Unwin.

Wright, G.H. von. (1990) *A Portrait of Wittgenstein as a Young Man*. Oxford: Basil Blackwell.

Young, D.A.B. (1994) 'Ramanujan's illness.' *Notes and Records of the Royal Society of London* 48, 107–119.

Acknowledgments

The Author and publisher gratefully acknowledge the permission granted to reproduce the copyright material in this book.

Extracts in Chapter 1 from *Michelangelo: A Lesson in Anatomy* by James Beck. Copyright © 1975 Phaidon Press Limited. Used by permission of Phaidon Press Limited.

Extracts in Chapter 16 from *Simone Weil* by Francine du Plessix Gray, published by Weidenfeld & Nicolson, a division of The Orion Publishing Group.

Extracts in Chapter 18 from *Beautiful Shadow: A Life of Patricia Highsmith* by Andrew Wilson. Copyright © Bloomsbury Publishing 2003. Used by permission of Bloomsbury Publishing.

Every reasonable effort has been made to trace copyright holders and to obtain their permission for the use of copyright material. The publisher apologizes for any errors or omissions in the above list and would be grateful for notification of any corrections or additions. Every effort will be made to promptly incorporate them in future reprints or editions of this book.